Discipling Music Ministry

Twenty-First Century Directions

Calvin M. Johansson

HENDRICKSON
PUBLISHERS
PEABODY, MASSACHUSETTS 01961-3473

Copyright © 1992 by Hendrickson Publishers, Inc.
P. O. Box 3473
Peabody, Massachusetts, 01961–3473

Printed in the United States of America

ISBN 0–943575–52–4

Library of Congress Cataloging-in-Publication Data

Johansson, Calvin M.
   Discipling music ministry: twenty-first century directions /
Calvin M. Johansson
       p.   cm.
   ISBN 0–943575–52–4 (pbk.)
   1. Music in churches. 2. Church music—United States.
I. Title.
ML3001.J63 1992
264′.7—dc20   92–11694
                                                      CIP
                                                      MN

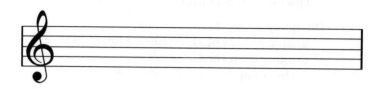

Table of Contents

Preface

Robert Novak, in a speech to the Notre Dame Club of Chicago on January 24, 1990, stated that the twentieth century "was perhaps the worst century our planet has yet endured—spectacular advancements in science and technology obscured by evil pure and unadorned."[1] It was a time of fundamental change. Political, social, and economic shifts were overshadowed by the creeping awareness that the basic presuppositions which had governed life were somehow outmoded and no longer viable. A new moral ethic was accepted as normative.

The church was deeply affected by these changes. Though often ineffective, its mission compromised and truncated by a well-meaning accommodation to culture, it carried on. Much church music (denominational as well as that of mass evangelism, certain parachurch organizations, and the charismatic and renewal movements) often unwittingly absorbed some of the less noble traits of our changing society. As a result, this music tended to reinforce the very values the church professed unacceptable.

But survival is not enough! We want to win the world. To do that will require a reevaluation of much of what we presently take for granted—even in the music of the church. The immediacy of facing into the twenty-first century presses us to begin without delay. A change in direction is needed.

The present volume attempts such redirection. *Discipling Music Ministry: Twenty-first Century Directions* reviews the past, evaluates the present, and suggests a course for the future—the way of discipline. The book takes the position that faith and works are interactive. The gospel is not communicated solely by the texts of church music. Church music proclaims the gospel through the actual music itself! The art form (music) is far more influential and powerful in affirming or denying lived-out faith than we commonly believe. Therefore we need a heightened awareness of what the notes, rhythms, and harmonies of our church music imply.

The word "discipling" in the title *Discipling Music Ministry* is intended to be both verbal and adjectival. On the one hand, as a verb, "discipling" acts upon the phrase "music ministry"; it *does* something to music ministry. The music ministry itself is "discipled"; ministry is the *receiver* of "discipling" action. We must discover what specific musical characteristics and traits, what musical vocabulary, what kinds and styles of music will result in a disciplined music. That disciplined music, in turn, causes ministry to be discipled insofar as such music is incorporated into the music program. Music ministry is discipled by adopting a music of discipline.

On the other hand, as an adjective, "discipling" describes a type of music ministry, one in which music ministry is the *giver* of "discipling" action. Music ministry modified by the adjective "discipling" shows that this type of music ministry is itself an agent of discipleship. That is, the primary function of a "discipling music ministry" is the training of the believer. The specific goal of that training or discipline, as well as suggestions for implementing such discipline, is the subject of this book.

Continuing where my *Music & Ministry: A Biblical Counterpoint* (Hendrickson Publishers, 1984) left off, the present volume will serve to expand the vision of the reader concerning the place church music has in the discipling process. After all, the great commission does not command us to make weaklings, but disciples. The music which disciples is the church music of the future.

Notes

1. Robert Novak from a speech delivered on January 24, 1990, to the Notre Dame Club of Chicago.

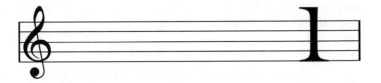

Congregations, Pastors, and Musicians

Discipling Music Ministry: Twenty-first Century Directions deals with the music ministry of the local church, the pastoral ministry of music. Hence our investigation will be limited to concerns which touch upon such ministry. We must identify the people who participate in the local church's music program as well as review the purposes for which music is used. Eventually we will validate and substantiate the discipling aspect of music ministry.

Music ministry at its best is a cooperative venture among congregation, pastor, and musician. Though each has its own particular role to play, a concerted effort toward a common goal not only makes its actual achievement more likely, but produces an esprit de corps absolutely essential to healthy corporate life. The end result is a dynamic spirituality seldom achieved any other way. Congregations, pastors, and musicians need to know that pastoral music ministry is relational and interdependent.

Congregations

Congregations are, of course, the focal point of music ministry. Everything that is composed, planned, practiced, and performed is for their benefit. All church music therefore must be attuned to the congregation. The assembly's importance may be noted in the following popular uses for church music: church music as textual information, church music as utilitarian function, and church music as offering.

Church Music as Textual Information

Church music as textual information exists to give religious witness via the text of a song. The emphasis is placed on immediate and direct communication. Texts are usually simple, often in the first person, and frequently experiential. The music to which they are set is popular in nature. Examples are: "Saved, Saved!"[1] "He Touched Me,"[2] and "Heaven Came Down and Glory Filled My Soul."[3]

Such witness music has a built-in proclivity toward the musical standards of popular culture. As a matter of fact, the first hurdle in the successful use of such songs is finding those which have a likeable music. In choosing what pleases people, musicians, like other popular communicators, keep the taste of their "audiences" in the forefront of their thinking. Music as textual information is successful to the extent that musicians choose songs that are easily understood, relevant, and enjoyable. Unless it considers the assembly's musical or topical preferences, message music does not succeed.

Church Music as Utilitarian Function

Another common practice is to use church music as utilitarian function. Music is regarded as an instrument, a tool, a facilitator, a mechanism for serving utilitarian ends. For example, music is often enlisted as a means of creating atmosphere, generating congregational praise, and celebrating liturgy. It covers the noise of walking and talking. It fills uncomfortable silences. Background music "enhances" prayers, scripture readings, and altar services. Its worth is believed to lie in its ability to fulfill a function.

The purpose of church music as utilitarian function is to service the assembly. If music is a means of accomplishing some functional or practical end, that end is invariably caught up in what is perceived to be of benefit to the congregation. If it is suspected that a particular use of music does not benefit the listeners, or is not congregationally hospitable, or is not consonant with their inclination and outlook, it will eventually be discarded. Functional church music is a music "for the people."

Church Music as Offering

In addition to seeing music as textual information and as utilitarian function, some see church music as an offering. That is, music is felt to be a sacrificial act, an offering to God. One branch of thought holds that music as offering is a matter of attitude. Personal in nature, it is offered from the heart of the individual performer directly to the heart of God. Popularized by the charismatic and renewal movements, music is often described as "ministering unto the Lord" or "praising the Lord." Emphasis is placed upon individual "heart-felt" worship. The intense devotional attitude of the participant is its distinguishing mark. A second branch emphasizes the quality of the music. We are admonished to give God the very best of our talents and abilities, the first-fruits of the work of our hands. The objective goodness of the musical composition as well as the artistry of the performance are of paramount importance.

At first glance, both of these branches of church music as offering seem to disregard the collective nature of Christian worship. Yet it should be acknowledged that a certain congregational awareness on the part of the director must be present. If, in worship, singing praises directly to God by each individual person is stressed, it is necessary that the music be chosen on the basis of the congregation's (that is, each person's) ability and partiality. If music is chosen without carefully considering the congregation, the musical praise will probably be a failure. Music the assembly loathes or is too difficult to sing will not likely become a vehicle of heart-felt worship! If, however, a great deal of importance is given to the quality of the musical offering, the music being given to God on behalf of the congregation, the congregation must still be considered. Without vicarious participation of the assembly, such musical offerings are essentially meaningless within the context of the gathered community. The musical offering must still be chosen largely on the basis of the congregation's ability to apprehend it.

All three emphases—church music as textual information, as utilitarian function, and as offering—are built around the congregation. This is a circumstance not generally appreciated by the average parishioner. It is often unjustly presumed that music directors choose music and design music programs on the basis of their personal tastes and preferences; any correspondence between what music directors choose and the music congregations prefer is thought to be purely coincidental. While this is certainly possible, it cannot be substantiated on any large scale. Church music without congregational involvement and support founders. Musical decisions must be made with the congregation in mind.

People and Musician

Congregations, then, have power: the power of their musical preferences, of the purse, of cooperation and goodwill. But there is more to say. The musician's role is not one of simply providing musical satisfaction for a powerful assembly. The prophetic character of music ministry may very well necessitate going against the grain of popular trends. The prophetic role of music has strong pastoral implications. Musicians, as ministers, respond to what they believe their congregation's well-being requires. When the musician's conscience, sensitized to those requirements, dictates a course of action the people find unappetizing, congregations must realize that such decisions are made not to spite them, but out of concern for them. In reality, responsible decisions, even unpopular ones, demonstrate the power that congregations have over music ministry. The gathered assembly always stands in the forefront of the church musician's decision-making processes.

When trust exists between musician and people, a mutually beneficial relationship results. The music director nurtures the congregation, and the congregation responds affirmatively to that nurture. People's attitudes toward the director's efforts can be helped by the knowledge that church music's purpose goes far beyond the limits usually assumed (i.e., its practical function). Spiritual health and character may be built up or torn down, helped or hindered, strengthened or weakened by music. Church music has the potential for operating on a plane far above the pragmatic or aesthetic philosophies that drive so much church music making. Without the congregation's awareness of the higher purposes of church music, misunderstanding between musician and people easily results. Only a modicum of ministry will then be possible.

The assembly's major contribution to this cooperative venture is a teachable spirit. Musicians know that congregations are seldom perfect; teaching is needed. But in order for that teaching to be successful, what is needed, above everything else, is a willingness on the part of the congregation to be taught. Responding to and submitting to newly understood truth and believing God's hand to be at work in making the assembly after the image of God's own Son are marks of a teachable people. Without these attitudes progress cannot be made.

A New Direction

Another plane of ministering through music, different in emphasis from church music as information, utility, or offering, is explored in the following chapters. Comprehending this plane of ministry will go a long way toward helping congregations give that cooperation so necessary for the development of a deeper music ministry. In some instances this may have already begun, though with a sense of congregational apathy and remoteness. Perhaps there has been no overt explanation of what is being attempted. If this is the case, the following chapters will articulate and clarify the new direction. Explaining the spiritual aims and objectives of the music program as well as demonstrating the musical methodology to be implemented ensure a degree of cooperation between musician and people unattainable any other way.

Pastors

Pastoral Authority

Pastors greatly influence the music program. Their influence may not be as primary as that of the congregation, but it is certainly more immediate and direct. The degree to which pastors exercise control is directly related to a variety of issues: church polity, the relative abilities of pastor and music director, the size of the parish, and the pastor's interest, psychological make-up, philosophy of ministry, creative ability, and talent as an administrator. Whatever a pastor's natural inclination might be, almost all church polity requires that the chief or senior pastor oversee the music program in some way and act as the liaison between the director and the specific governing body of the church, be it board, session, vestry, or council.

The degree of control pastors exercise over the music program varies considerably. No two situations are ever exactly alike, with as many varieties of pastoral control over church music as there are pastors and music directors. Whatever the specific case, it is safe to say that most pastors assume more control than directors prefer; directors, in turn, usually want more control than pastors prefer.

Pastors and Musicians

Some pastors give church music an occasional cursory glance, others believe music a necessary bother (the less of it, the better), some show a modicum of interest, others an all-consuming or even dictatorial interest. Some pastors take the hired hand approach toward musicians; others could care less about them and the whole musical undertaking. And worst of all, some pastors know nothing (or very little) about church music, either technically or theologically and philosophically, yet they exercise arbitrary control over matters which are beyond their knowledge and understanding.

Certainly many stories of bitter disagreements have their basis in fact. Some stem from imagined slights, others from legitimate complaints. Some are too offensive to repeat, others too petty; all are unworthy of our Lord Jesus Christ. How can a congregation be expected to act Christ-like when its leaders act unchristianly, without charity or justice?

Fortunately most pastors are genuinely interested in the welfare of church music and church musicians. Some understand music to be inextricably linked with worship, and they champion it at every turn. There are even ministers who assume music to be worship, not merely a decoration or an accoutrement to worship. These recognize the difference between music as ministry and music as entertainment. They realize the implicit biblical injunctions which give music a place of importance in the corporate life of God's people (see 1 Chronicles 6; 2 Chronicles 5; Nehemiah 12; Psalm 149; Matthew 26:30; 1 Corinthians 14:26; Ephesians 5:19). They have the self-confidence necessary for employing knowledgeable musicians and delegating to them the authority for making the music program the very best it can be within the context of a particular congregational setting.

Recently the office of musician has undergone a subtle shift which has altered somewhat the relationship between pastors and musicians. Influences such as the political democratization of whole societies, the societal importance of individual independence, the Second Vatican Council (1962–1965), and the relatively recent emphasis on the ministry of the laity have given rise to a church environment in which a shared or collaborative type of staff ministry has evolved. Musical leaders are charged with the development of the gifts of the gathered community and enjoy the freedom to exercise their leadership as they believe appropriate. Such an arrangement has the effect of somewhat lessening the autocratic control of the pastor and giving a wider scope of responsibility to the musician.

Nevertheless pastors still have, in most situations, the general oversight of the music program. For them to abandon all leadership does great harm. Without their hearty support, warranted by the close relationship between music and worship, the church music program becomes but one of many optional ministries dependent upon congregational preference. But the music ministry is much too significant to worship to be optional. The general attitude of the pastor will, in great measure, determine its relative importance. Strong clergy involvement, without arbitrary control, is the best type of pastoral leadership for advancing the work of an informed ministry of music.

Pastoral Understanding of Music Ministry

Seminaries seldom prepare clergy for general oversight of the music program. If there is training at all, it usually is in the area of practics (leading songs, chanting liturgy, reading music) or in historical study of music and worship. Unfortunately, the theological underpinnings of church music are seldom addressed. Without properly comprehending the nature of music ministry, the clergy's potential for crippling it is enormous.

Two areas need addressing. First, like congregations, pastors need an understanding of the deeper spiritual ramifications of church music. Without question the texts of our church music are significant. But it is the implications of music apart from text that have, in many ways, an even greater significance. It is precisely this fact of which most pastors (and to a lesser degree, musicians) are unaware. If pastors are to exercise competent leadership in encouraging and nurturing music ministry, then they must strengthen their understanding of its effect upon spirituality. Too often clergy have been satisfied with the philosophical vagaries and trite platitudes of well-meaning generalities! Though sounding impressive, such philosophies are often clouded by wordiness and are essentially meaningless! But as general overseers, pastors simply need insight into what it is that gives certain music the potential for strengthening spirituality, and other types of music the potential for weakening it.

A second area which needs addressing is church music methodology. Agreement between pastors and musicians on the spiritual goals of music making in the church is relatively easy to achieve: people should be loving, exercise the fruits of the Spirit, show strong moral character, cultivate habits of mature worship, and be a people who live out their faith in a most inhospitable world. Almost every music director and pastor would not only agree with these goals but would zealously promulgate them.

The battle between musicians and pastors becomes most vexatious when, in opposition to the musician's methodology, the pastor dictates the musical methodology for achieving spiritual goals. If it is true that arbitrary decisions concerning music-making by a pastor who sees no relationship between music and spirituality are difficult to live with, how much more grievous are decisions by a pastor who agrees on spiritual matters with the musician but who then undoes the musician's ministry by insisting on musical practices that the musician knows will make their common spiritual goals largely unattainable. What a sad, but all too prevalent, situation!

One purpose of this book is to heighten the pastor's awareness of the spiritual implications of the church's melodies, rhythms, and harmonies. Christian discipleship is developed and exercised through the use of a comparatively narrow range of musical choices. Though the twentieth-century church has not always chosen wisely in this regard, our faith gives us hope that the church of the next century will do better.

Musicians

Church Music-making

Professional church musicians work heavily on the mechanics of music-making: correct fingering, clear conducting gestures, proper vocal placement, correct notes, exact cut-offs, meticulous articulation, and accurate rhythms. Through these and a host of other technical and interpretive details, they bring alive the composer's intentions. They make music.

As facilitators of amateur music-making, however, church musicians know that volunteerism, at its best, depends heavily upon an alive, vigorous, and exuberant enthusiasm. Technical brilliance becomes secondary. Such is the case for the Sunday school men's choir, handbell choir, orchestra, and the other ensembles of the music program. Energy and enthusiasm count far more than technical correctness. They measure the music program's vitality.

Nevertheless, the work of musicians requires them to strive continually for as much technical excellence as possible. In their practices with the parish choir, soloists, and instrumental ensembles, directors are confronted with less technical prowess than most music demands. Hence, much of their time is spent drilling notes, correcting rhythms, and teaching vowel unification. To be a music director means to work at the technique of making music. Church musicians are artisans.

Implications of Compositional Choice on Ministry

Spending so much time and effort rehearsing technically needy amateurs gives the average church musician a mindset that is more concerned with performance quality than compositional quality. Excellence of production, not excellence of composition, is emphasized. This is understandable. Music in the church does not purport to be "professional." It is largely a matter of marshalling parish volunteers into musical undertakings commensurate with their ability. It is not that directors do not carefully choose the musical material for their music programs; rather, their attention in choosing is usually riveted to practical matters: difficulty level, musical appeal, or available vocal and instrumental resources. Questions concerning musical value and the spiritual implications of the music itself retreat to the background. Compositional accessibility, not compositional integrity, is, for most musicians, the crux of the matter.

There are other reasons why many church musicians tend to embrace a pragmatic approach to music-making. The twentieth-century tendency toward extreme subjectivism, the failure to integrate faith and life, and the lackadaisical attitude toward values all have a part in making the musician's decisions less thoughtful and more reflexive. Choice becomes largely a conditioned response to the cultural values adopted by a particular church or denomination.

As we have noted, however, the point of music in the church and the point of the musician's pastoral work are their spiritual impact on the life of the congregation. Musicians have a prophetic role to play in the assembly, which makes them ministers in the highest sense of the word. Ordained or not, church musicians have a call to ministry.

Ministry is not just sacerdotal functioning or some fuzzy notion of "helping others" or a kind of maudlin sentimentality. Ministry is salt and light, active and dynamic. Music ministry, as it is faithful to its prophetic role, helps shape the spirituality of every member of the assembly. It is pastoral, its vision a faith-building vision. Music becomes the agent of prophetic ministry just as words are the agent of the preaching ministry. Notes are not an end, but a means. Musical composition touches the ultimate concerns of ministry.

The Musician's Teaching Ministry

Church musicians need to be teachers. Even when they choose music for its spiritual character, its full spiritual potential will be lost unless the congregation recognizes its spiritual dimension. Playing the right music without reflecting upon its ultimate meaning is just as undesirable as playing the wrong music for the right reasons. The assembly needs teaching in musical/spiritual concepts. Once more, if the congregation lacks any idea of what gives music significant spiritual meaning, the full spiritual potential of the music is dissipated. Teaching is needed to give scope and definition to the lofty purposes to which church music is called.

The role of teacher is a significant change from how most musicians, congregations, and pastors view the work of church musicians. Usually, directors are hired to produce a commodity—music. In addition, their contractual arrangements required them to oversee the administration of the music program and occasionally perform other tasks peripheral to worship. Church musicians as teachers, therefore, is no doubt a relatively new idea for many congregations, pastors, and musicians. The church, existing in a society generally not well versed in the musical arts or in apprehending the more elusive relationship between music and spiritual life, needs to change the musician's portfolio. For a congregation's own good the director's work demands regular and systematic teaching. Congregations and pastors must also provide a convenient forum for such teaching to take place. Midweek service, Christian education, Sunday morning sermon time, or a few minutes prior to the beginning of worship are possibilities.

The teaching ministry of church musicians is addressed further in the following pages. Little will be said about reading music, widening repertoire, or learning to appreciate music as an art. Rather, music's influence upon spiritual formation will be stressed. This aspect of church music is in the most need of shoring up.

Notes

1. Jack P. Scholfield, "Saved, Saved!," *The Hymnal for Worship and Celebration* (Waco: Word Music, 1986), 530.

2. William J. Gaither, "He Touched Me," *The Hymnal for Worship and Celebration* (Waco: Word Music, 1986), 504.

3. John W. Peterson, "Heaven Came Down and Glory Filled My Soul," *The Hymnal for Worship and Celebration* (Waco: Word Music, 1986), 495.

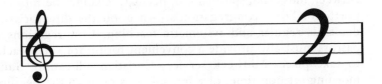

The Purpose of Church Music

The Importance of Purpose

The fundamental question concerning music ministry is: What is the purpose of church music? All other questions pale next to this one. Music is so adaptable and multi-faceted that it fills almost any role it is assigned. To keep it from uses which are inconsequential, if not erroneous, and to enlist it instead to its fullest potential, we must settle the question of purpose. The answer will determine the shape and content of music ministry.

Variety of Purposes

All of us have experienced a variety of church music uses, good and bad. Most of these fall into the three categories given in chapter 1: church music as textual information, utilitarian function, and offering. Music carries text, it is used for preludes, offertories, and postludes, and it is a vehicle of praise and worship. Music covers silence and noise, generates moods, accompanies liturgical action, and is contemplated purely for its aesthetic beauty. Songs are even sung for recreation ("Let's change our positions and stand, singing hymn 121, first and last stanzas.")!

For many congregations, pastors, and musicians, these are the prime reasons for which church music exists. Such viewpoints reflect a superficial naiveté or a contrived or mechanistic calculation. Even though done with the very best of intentions, music may still be inappropriate, even contrary, to church music's ultimate goal simply because its deeper purpose and the methodology for achieving it have never been ascertained. Church music is, without question, functional. But fulfilling just any function will not do. Function must grow out of a well-conceived, biblically based objective. Knowing that objective, more than anything else, should determine the use to which music is put.

Purpose as Reflective of the Church's Mission

Obviously the purpose of church music should be determined by the nature and mission of the church itself. That is to say, the supernatural should determine the natural; the theological, the musical. The spiritual dimension of life in God should afford music a purpose commensurate with that dimension.

At first glance such an assumption would seem to be a foregone conclusion. Surely it is reasonable to assume that various aspects of the church's life, whether art, architecture, literature, music, human relationships, morality, or business practice, would be affected in their very essence by what the church teaches—outworkings of our doctrinal belief. But this is not necessarily so.

Often what we believe as Christians and what we do as Christians are in conflict. We would hope that Sunday's sermon would be applied to Monday's relationships. Unfortunately, this does not always happen. Theoretically, the church stands for justice, morality, and holiness—biblical concepts that we wholeheartedly endorse, but troublesome to put into practice. The church as an institution and Christians as individuals have often been guilty of inconsistencies between faith and practice.

When it comes to expressions such as art, architecture, and music, items a bit more elusive in their connection to doctrine than ethics or morality, biblical concepts are rarely taken into account. The doctrine of creation, the *Imago Dei*, incarnation, or stewardship are seldom applied to church music. We may show concern that its use be liturgically correct or scan its texts for theological accuracy, but we seldom apply theological truth to the music itself (its melody, harmony, and rhythm). Hence the actual music of ministry is cast adrift to be influenced by forces other than that which it is supposed to represent—Christianity. Not many congregations, pastors, and musicians realize religious art forms need to be shaped by faith.

Church music, then, should have a purpose reflective of the church, a purpose derived from the church's mission. No other source will do. If a carpenter's purpose is to build houses, then the tools employed must be designed to accomplish that task. Likewise the musician must select musical tools that will accomplish the church's purpose. Church ministry and church music share a common objective, the former determinatively influencing the latter.

The Church's Mission—Christian Maturation

All Christians are fully adopted sons or daughters of God. Nothing more needs to be done to complete their Christian citizenship. They are heirs to all the privileges and responsibilities of a child of God.

New Christians are immature. Though fully part of God's family, they are like children, incomplete in the sense that they are undeveloped. But God, as Father, desires for them a holistic maturity. And the moment Christians are born into the kingdom, the process of maturation begins. At first we take "milk"; later, "meat." Becoming mature means becoming what God intends.

Maturity is not an accoutrement to the Christian life, one of many noble characteristics for which Christians strive. It is not something optional which is added to the virtues of love, kindness, gentleness, and patience; to the keeping of the moral, ethical, and social law; or to habits of personal piety, good works, stewardship, and intercessory prayer. Maturity is not an addition to Christian character at all. Rather, we exhibit Christian characteristics to the extent that we are mature. Maturity is the degree to which we have become like our Lord. It is a lifelong quest.

God ordained the church to be a source of his grace. Thus, it is the church which, through example and instruction, is best fitted for helping make life the profitable schoolhouse in which God's larger purposes for us will be accomplished. Differing church bodies dispense that grace in any number of ways. But all churches share three universal activities: evangelism, teaching, and worship. Each contributes in its own way to our becoming God's children in the fullest sense of the term.

Evangelism—The Beginning of Christian Maturation

Evangelism endeavors to bring new believers into the kingdom of God. Until that point, the process of Christian maturity cannot begin. Conversion is prerequisite to becoming all that God intends.

The general tone of a new convert's life in Christ is often set by the method used in the evangelistic encounter. It would be hoped that the method is congruous with God's plan for his children, a plan of a holistic maturity. It is inconsistent, and, frankly, dishonest to use (in the name of Christ of all things!) means that in themselves are not discipled by their goals. How people are brought into the kingdom of God surely affects their expectation of what is to follow. If their expectations are not fulfilled, they tend either to fall away or to live immaturely.

Though the intent may be good, to brainwash or propagandize men and women into the kingdom of God is at least naive if not unscrupulous. When the conversion method is incompatible with the purpose of becoming a Christian in the first place, great harm comes to the overall building up of the kingdom. It would be better for evangelistic forms to reflect the type of life to which Christianity calls us. For example, nothing is gained by entertaining people into the kingdom, musically speaking, only to have them jolted into the reality that the Christian life is not an entertainment at all. Disciplined evangelistic methods give a more realistic start to the new saint. One's birthing process should be a foretaste of the lifelong faith walk toward maturity, which is God's goal for every Christian.

Teaching—A Maturation Help

A second main activity of the church, teaching, takes many forms: catechism classes, Sunday school, Bible school, special study courses, portions of church worship such as hymns, scripture lessons, and sermons, classes for church membership, baptism, and confirmation. All of these have the potential for furthering and improving the spiritual walk of the Christian. They help us mature.

In keeping with what we have said about evangelism, it is apropos to note once more that the form of the instruction (as well as the content) must not work against the ultimate goal of the instruction—maturity in Christ. The best instructional forms are neither frivolous, irrelevant, nor trivial. If the aim is to mature the Christian, instruction should be designed in such a way that maturity results. Poorly crafted stories that use inappropriate language and faulty structure, or emphasize inconsequential points, may be fun for children, but they do not result in sound Christian education. Fashioning the form to match the goal will better insure its attainment. Any music used in teaching ought to help the student grow and develop. Music which is immature for people at a particular level of development does little for promoting growth.

Worship—A Maturing Process

Worship, the third of the three main activities of the church, has gained much more attention than the other two because it is the single most important activity of Christians. All churches agree that the worship of almighty God is central to the faith. As a matter of fact, so innate is the religious urge that anthropologists are hard pressed to find societies which do not affirm the sacred in some way.[1]

In Christian worship, God and humanity meet. The redeemed give glory, honor, and praise to God because he is worthy of our praise. We ascribe worth to a deserving Creator. We praise him for who he is and for what he has done—a celebration of the whole Christ-event from creation to the second coming. We do this in symbol and sign, word and sacrament, praise and prayer, sound and silence. Our focus is entirely on the Godhead. We are caught up in the universal activity God has intended for all of creation, an activity which will continue forever.

Though worship belongs to God, it has an effect upon the worshiper, determined largely by its quality and design. We plan it. We craft it. We execute it. As a result, this which we fashion, the work of our hands, molds us in its own image. Worship itself has an outcome which is directed back to the believer. Though not particularly self-evident, in large measure, worship determines the quality of our walk with God. If it is immature, then the congregation becomes immature. The shape of our worship shapes us.

Worship Content Influences the Worshiper's Maturity

Humanity's basic sin concerns the self: pride, egocentricity, disobedience. Down deep our natural inclination is to live as though life revolves around us, a notion given credence by much contemporary psychological and philosophical thought. We become the center of our own reference.

The self-centeredness of a newborn child is, of course, a sign of immaturity. Infants have no concerns except for getting what they want: milk, a blanket, or a dry diaper. They are motivated by their own desires.

As they grow and develop, their behavior changes. They begin to realize that others must be considered. Adults do not exist simply to cater to their every whim! The child learns that there are things which are acceptable and unacceptable, things which they can do and cannot do. Limits are put on them. We teach them to put others ahead of themselves. As they become more and more socialized we say they are maturing.

A mark of maturity, then, is the decreasing importance of the self and the increasing importance of others. A person maturing is becoming selfless, not selfish; other-affirming, not self-affirming.

Similarly, true worship is an activity whose focus moves from the self to another. To the extent our worship focuses on God and shows a simultaneous lessening on self, worship matures the worshiper. Maturation is one of the results of a well-designed, heart-felt worship.

The component parts of the worship service, such as sermon, music, poetry, or creed, have the potential for helping to bring worshipers out of their natural state of egocentricity into a blossoming theocentric growth. We need to remember that the spotlight is not on "me" but on God. Pleasing the self, indulging the adamic nature, and gratifying the desires of one's own carnality countermand the intent of worship. The forms, be they architecture, text, music, space, admonition, poetry, symbol, art, or drama, can help or hinder. They can heighten people's awareness of themselves or heighten awareness of God, be oriented around the individual or God. Insofar as they diminish our selfism they are maturing agents. At their best they aid us in becoming what God calls us to be: men and women who are mature, who have left babyhood behind, whose works of praise fulfill the highest plan of God for his children—growing up.

The Purpose of Church Music—Christian Maturation

Following after the church's mission to foster Christian maturity through evangelism, teaching, and worship, it is logical to assume that in enabling men and women to praise God, music ministry's fundamental task is the maturing of the saints of God. That it has other functions does not diminish this important purpose. Actually it is in the execution of its other tasks, such as serving as musical settings for psalms, hymns, and canticles, or as preludes or postludes, or as anthems or solos, that its maturing processes are put into play. Here there can be no place for self-indulgence. If maturity is God's plan for his children, let congregations, pastors, and musicians cooperate by using music which will help enrich God's people. To its shame, the music of the church has often served to make Christians more immature than mature. That needs changing as we move into the twenty-first century.

In Summation

All three of the main activities of the church, evangelism, teaching, and worship, aim at maturing God's saints. Each in its own way serves to conform us increasingly to the perfect revelation of God, Jesus Christ. We begin our growing journey (evangelism), are taught along the way (teaching), and meet with God (worship) all for the purpose of achieving God's ends for his children. Though we are fully his sons and daughters at the new birth, he wants us to grow and develop. To do that takes dedication and perseverance. Every beneficial aid is utilized, including music.

That the three main activities of church life work toward maturing the Christian is an obvious and unmistakable indication that what is used as part of these activities (e.g., music) also advances that same cause. Such a goal for church music moves beyond what we have hitherto assumed or claimed—it goes right to the heart of God's purpose, helping mightily the process of holistic maturation. Depending upon the technical characteristics of music within a given cultural parameter, music can be one of maturity's strongest assets or one of its greatest liabilities.

If the church takes seriously God's plan for the maturation of his people, it must embrace that music which will help accomplish that goal. For music to neglect its maturing role is imprudent and negligent. Church music has the potential of being one of the most important ways of fulfilling God's desire for each of us. We must not allow the musical gift to be wasted.

Notes

1. Mircea Eliade, *The Sacred and the Profane: The Nature of Religion* (New York: Harcourt Brace Jovanovich, Publishers, 1959), 209, 223–32.

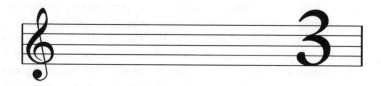

Culture

The Church and Culture

Congregations, pastors, and musicians, having apprehended church music's goal of Christian maturity, run head on into contemporary culture and trouble. The goal of church music is largely out of step with the march of society as a whole, resulting in tension between it and the cultural milieu. Moreover, the goal of church music and that of secular music are often incompatible, the latter being more in tune with worldly pursuits than with heavenly ones. The adoption and adaptation of secular music does not fulfill church music's overall purpose because it is incapable of doing so. Accommodating the gospel to culture is often a vexatious problem.

These things need further elucidation. The church is, of course, part of culture. It is but one of the innumerable things which make up the cultural background of a nation. Furthermore, the only way the church can get its work done is through culture. Language, music, and architecture are all cultural forms. These are the communicative means which encode God's message in terms understandable to the human race. The church, therefore, is a cultural entity which utilizes cultural tools to fulfill its mission.

But the church is also supra-cultural. That is, it is a body which purports to be above culture. It is, in short, a supernatural body, one through whom God acts upon the world through cultural forms. This is unique since no other institution can claim (from a Christian faith perspective) to be the channel through which the otherworldly impacts the worldly. The distinction of being above culture by virtue of having an authoritative word from outside of culture is the mark of the church's divine appointment.

Enculturation of the Gospel

The church has adopted uncritically many cultural expressions and has unwittingly weakened its witness. Artistic forms which lack aesthetic value do not convey biblical truth well. It is always advisable to be cautious when expressing the divine through the material, because the quality of an art form bears upon the accuracy with which the gospel is fleshed out. In our society, the pressing need to proclaim the truth has precipitated an often rash embracing of the pragmatic method: Whatever appears to work is used without regard for the means employed. The latest faddish forms are then appropriated without judicious evaluation. The temporal (musical forms) is taken at face value without realizing that the form in question might have more in common with the powers of darkness than with the powers of light.

The only way that Christians can live out the Christ life is in terms of culture. We cannot separate ourselves from the material world in which we live. All the things we do have spiritual significance and are interwoven into the very warp and woof of life. One cannot be loving without being loving in relation to someone. A Christian's love, coming from God who is beyond culture, must be worked out in terms of culture. To be loving is to act loving. John said: "This is how we know what love is: Jesus Christ laid down his life for us. And we ought to lay down our lives for our brothers" (1 John 3:16, NIV). He then goes on to explain in cultural terms exactly what this love might mean by asking a rhetorical question: "If anyone has material possessions and sees his brother in need but has no pity on him, how can the love of God be in him?" (1 John 3:17, NIV). The spiritual (love) must be clothed in the material (perhaps a cloak). Christian charity is worked out cultural manifestations—material expressions of the gospel message.

The place and quality that works of art should have in our Christian cultural complex are not as apparent as charity or the need for holiness, for example. Just which style, aesthetic value, and general ethos church music should be endowed with continues to be a matter of conjecture. The fuzziness of our thinking is compounded by the fact that we live in an increasingly secularized society which almost routinely dichotomizes the sacred and the secular, and which does not believe church art to be within the parameters of theological imperatives. Nevertheless the arts are not only here to stay; they are more powerful than ever. Contemporary culture is art-filled.

The Arts Lead Culture

Art Forms Influence Culture

The arts shape our world more than any other aspect of culture: movies, magazines, radio, television, records, newspapers, video, literature, and all types of music have a leverage second to none. Until the twentieth century a case could be made for treating the arts as reflectors of culture. That is no longer a plausible explanation of the position the arts enjoy in society. Becoming much more powerful and more pervasive, they exert an influence formerly reserved for philosophy, theology, and more recently, science. Contemporary artists "represent what is probably the most powerful single force molding cultural patterns and society [sic] attitudes."[1] Understandably, such a view might be granted people like Jean-Paul Sartre, Samuel Beckett, or Joseph Heller, who through language inculcate specific philosophical positions in their literature or drama. But all artists invariably have a philosophical position underlying their work. Inherent even in formal aspects (notes, lines, shapes, harmonies, space, or silence), the basic visionary presuppositions of the artist are communicated to the audience. People, in turn, are changed or influenced through their perception of and interaction with the art work.

Artists

Artists are image makers since they change the way we perceive the world. They impart values, beliefs, and perceptions, providing focus, drive, and appeal to the symbols and myths by which society lives.[2] For example, with the advent of "rock 'n' roll" after the second world war, popular music demonstrated an incredible power to alter the moral code, social structure, and aesthetic sensibility of young people. The statement of the Beatles that, "Our music is capable of causing emotional instability, disorganized behavior, rebellion, and even revolution"[3] is not unwarranted. Though rock music is one of the more visible and more powerful artistic expressions affecting culture, all artists have had some effect. Cage, de Kooning, Lennon, and Camus have each had a part to play in shaping society.

The media arts, with their instant communication potential, have also been influential in shaping society. Movies, television, and video have accustomed us to less emphasis on substance and greater emphasis on image. Their values and standards, constantly promoted larger than life, become society's own. Individuals in the arts have become the prophets of modern culture.

The Power of the Arts

Perhaps it is a bit too strong to take literally the statement, "Give me the making of the songs of a nation, and I care not who makes its laws."[4] But it contains a profound truth. While a C major chord, the color green, or the word "but" are quite neutral, put together within a framework of like grammatical elements, they emerge as an entity with a point of view. We may not recognize it, but it is there. All art works and media presentations make statements: they enlarge or diminish, ennoble or debase, enrich or rob us. Although they cannot force us to be what we do not wish to be, they influence us in a manner more powerful than any dictatorial edict, since art forms alter us from within. As they affect our minds and hearts, we cannot help being changed by the repetition of lyrics and music, the textual point of view, and its musical ethos. We become that which we assimilate. Indeed, "What people learn best today is not what their teachers think they teach or what their preachers think they preach, but what their *culture* in fact *cultivates*."[5] The presuppositions which drive the arts become those which drive our families, schools, governments, and businesses, instructing our thinking, molding our reasoning, and influencing our judgment. No one is exempt from their spell—and nothing is off limits to their probing.

The potential the arts have for shaping us in their image is understandable. Studies show that most young people listen to rock music, for example, about 10,500 hours for the six-year period between grades seven and twelve, close to thirty percent more time than they spend in school![6] In 1986 more money was spent on admissions to cultural events than on sporting events, according to the National Endowment for the Humanities.[7] The exposure we have to artistic forms is extraordinary. The values, standards, morality, and ethics of all of us, but especially our youth, are in the hands of the artists. We tend to become what the form and content of our art works present. They have more to do with the actual formation and daily working out of belief than anything else. Whether it be cinema, television, literature, or church music, the artist's messages do not go unheeded.

The Influence of Rock

The music of our culture which has most influenced late twentieth-century church music is rock music. It is unquestionably the most popular form of music in the world. In fact when two social scientists at Temple University decided to do a study on rock, the project had to be abandoned because no control group could be found among the student body who fulfilled the criteria of disliking it![8]

Rock is not only the most popular cultural phenomenon of the second half of the twentieth century, it is the single greatest propagator of the moral, ethical, social, and aesthetic revolution in which we find ourselves. The underlying philosophic assumptions of rock stem from romanticism and pantheism, according to Robert Pattison.[9] But the actual working presuppositions of its trend-setting composers are nihilistic (or some variant of it). Rock "is intended to broaden the generation gap [and] to alienate children from their parents" (Jefferson Airplane/Starship).[10] It promotes rebellion (Alice Cooper),[11] violence, and aggression (Allen Lanier).[12] According to "punk rock" manager Malcolm McLaren, rock 'n' roll is pagan, its true meaning: "sex, subversion and style."[13] The long-held values of biblical theism have been discarded for lyrics and music reflective of a "new morality." Rock glorifies drugs, illicit sex, and pornography; indeed, drugs and sex are the "premier dietary law of rock."[14] Speed, cocaine, marijuana, Seconal, morphine, LSD, and heroin use is matched by a like doping on sound and sight technology and a view of sex which is so putrid and obscene that most print media will not reproduce certain of the lyrics.[15] Rock music's appeal is a "barbaric appeal to sexual desire."[16] Indeed, the goal of rock, incredible as it may seem, is to "subsume the universe and become God."[17] God is "obliterated in a pantheist's cosmic orgasm."[18]

Rock's Musical and Textual Content

Much has been written about rock from the Christian standpoint, pro and con. Invariably its treatment has been superficial, especially by those who believe Christians should avoid the "secular" version of rock but embrace the "Christian" version. These evaluations have tended to be based on texts, life-styles of the artists, and the graphics of the music's packaging. Less has been said about the music itself.

The reason the music has largely gone unchallenged is the subjective notion that the notes, harmony, and rhythm of such songs contain no worldview, moral ethos, or life outlook. It is felt that music does not reflect a moral, philosophical, or theological position. Hence, the church has naively and simplistically split asunder the medium (music) and message (text). Some Christians have embraced the music of rock (or a derived version of it) while disavowing the texts! In fact, such a split is not feasible. Christian rock of whatever category is still rock since the message remains the same, now having moved from bars, dance halls, and clubs to the chancel. We have not only given nihilistic rockers a forum to peddle their wares, but we do it for them!

The music and texts of rock are products of the same presuppositions. The ethos generated by the characteristics of the music supports the meaning of the texts. "I am an anti-Christ, I am an anarchist." (Johnny Rotten)[19] Jim Morrison's philosophy is similar. "There are no rules, There are no laws."[20] The famous art historian H. R. Rookmaaker notes that a non-intellectual music emerged "with a thumping rhythm and shouting voices, each line and each beat full of the angry insult to all Western values, if these could be called values, of music or of culture or of behaviour."[21] He goes on, "Their protest is in their music itself as well as in the words, for anyone who thinks that this is all cheap and no more than entertainment has never used his ears."[22]

The substance and style of the music of rock songs are in keeping with their lyrical content. The sounds of the Anti-Nowhere League, de Sade, and Throbbing Gristle are just as lewd as the lyrics they use. Prince's "Purple Rain," Judas Priest's "Eat Me Alive," Motley Crue's "Ten Seconds to Love," and Sheena Easton's "Sugar Walls" are not just words put to any music. They are unified entities. Substituting more appropriate or decorous texts to the same music or musical style is of no consequence because the music will have its lewd say regardless of text.

The music of rock supports the repudiation of biblical standards by using combinations of sounds which are violent, mind-numbing, vulgar, raw, mesmerizing, rebellious, grossly repetitive, uncreative, undisciplined, and chaotic sounding. If listeners do not hear these things, it is because rock has dulled their aesthetic sensibilities. Rock's anarchist and vulgar approach to composition produces music which is tasteless, blunt, rude, indiscriminate, frenzied, and wild. Speaking of today's more raucous and abrasive pop music, violinist Isaac Stern fears "for the effect it has on thinking young minds. In some of this music, violence and the call to violence have become acceptable. It's not acceptable to me. I view the arts as freeing us from the slavery of our worst emotions. They're not a home for hatred."[23]

Either by design or default, consciously or unconsciously, the composer's view of reality affects the choice of material. The presuppositions of the composer are passed on to the listener via the music, and secondarily, through the words. These assumptions may come as mere suggestions, hints, or feelings and may be assimilated unknowingly. But they may also be eagerly and deliberately sopped up by those who know quite well what is going on. We cannot be so naive as to think that rock artists' views of life are kept to themselves since their art forms are but extensions of personal value systems. The most popular music of our culture is incompatible with Christian standards.

Culture Shapes the Church

The church is not exempt from culture's march. For example, the Roman Catholic Second Vatican Council (1962–1965), the Lambeth Conferences, and the numerous councils on world evangelism have all had to deal with the changes wrought by and challenges posed by twentieth-century culture. Whether it be a matter of apartheid, sexual conduct, ethics, or methodology in spreading the gospel, culture has had its say and the church has been affected.

There are many examples of this assault on historic church dogma. Among the most visible are those concerning pre-marital sex and homosexuality. That society has generally repudiated the church's traditional stance is a *fait accompli*. It was as if the church had little or no power in the matter because accepted standards, thousands of years old and clearly supported by holy scripture, were wiped clean from the mores of society with hardly a shrug. The arts led the way with the church impotent to stem the tide. About all it could do was guard the value system of its own faithful.

But even then the church was tempted by the allure of culture's changing standards. Accommodation with the world was broached: councils, meetings, and conventions convened to study the possible adoption of or adaptation to these changes. It was as if culture dictated not only the agenda, but the outcome as well. The church, like the children of Israel, found out that culture is not all that neutral. Baal is not dead.

Culture, then, has the potential for weakening the church. Secularizing influences touch every aspect of church life: its evangelism, teaching, and worship. Specific denominations find their individual stands on sex, lying, salvation, cheating, secret societies, charity, abortion, and school prayer under attack. From the folk mass to coke and potato chip communion to gospel entertainment, the church cannot wiggle free from its lovers' quarrel with the world.

Knowing Our Culture

Confronting the World

It is imperative for the church to recognize clearly what it is up against. We must get to know our opponent. In sports, wise playing decisions are always based upon knowing the strengths and weaknesses of the competitor. Baseball pitchers study their "little black books." Tennis players watch videos of their next challengers. Chess players meticulously study the previous matches of their adversaries. Knowledge of the opposition is essential to effective action.

The Old Testament prophets knew their opposition. With a keen understanding of the culture in which they lived they spoke out loudly and fiercely against the breaking of God's law. Isaiah proclaimed the coming judgment upon Israel because of its sin: Jeremiah warned Israel of the consequences of apostasy, and Malachi reminded the returned exiles that God would not tolerate disobedience from them anymore than he had from their forefathers.[24]

The New Testament also abounds with admonitions to beware of culture. Peter talks about the pollution and corruption in the world, John admonishes us to "love not the world neither the things that are in the world," and Paul reminds us that we need to be delivered from the "rulers of the darkness of this world," and we are not to be "conformed to this world."[25] It is the world—not as earth itself, but as a system bent against God—which is our opponent.

To be effective in this continuing struggle with culture, we, like the men and women of the Old and New Testaments, must understand our culture for what it is. If we are blind to the spirit of our age, innocently sopping up the mores and cultural patterns of an unchristian society, our character and witness become weakened. Defenses break down and before we realize it we are believing, saying, doing, understanding, and acting like the unregenerate. We become a small cog driven by a very large and powerful cultural wheel which slowly, methodically, and inexorably drives us to do its worldly bidding. But to be forewarned is to be forearmed. An understanding of our culture saves us from an indiscriminate acceptance of it.

Current Philosophical Changes

As age old philosophical foundations crumble they are replaced by new ones which are quite different, even radically so, from those espoused by a theistic worldview. From these philosophies emanate a spirit which permeates the entire culture. Whether it be some form of nihilism or a fresh twist of the New

Age movement, it is the duty of the church to recognize the general tone or spirit of the changes wrought by our culture.

The philosophical changes we are speaking about did not happen overnight; nor have they gone unnoticed by scholars and theologians. The brilliant Dr. Will Herberg stated in 1968 that: "Today's culture comes very close to becoming a non-moral, normless culture."[26] Dr. Allan Bloom recently issued a similar analysis of culture with warnings on relativistic values.[27] The wider culture has adopted philosophical assumptions that are fundamentally, essentially, and even radically opposed to those which have served Western society so well for two thousand years. Culture, in large measure, is no longer beholden to a law higher than itself!

The Church's Mandate

It is difficult to cut against the grain. But that is the church's mandate. We are not to find a comfortable berth in the world. Rather, we are to birth men and women into the kingdom of God so that God's intent for each person might be accomplished. That takes the ability to steer around the emplacements erected by a world which believes in its own autonomy. John said it well: "Never give your hearts to this world or to any of the things in it. A man cannot love the Father and love the world at the same time. For the whole world system, based as it is on men's primitive desires, their greedy ambitions and the glamor of all they think splendid, is not derived from the Father at all, but from the world itself" (1 John 2:15–16, PHILLIPS).

Only by understanding culture's philosophical assumptions will the church be able to effectively combat them. Questionable presuppositions, acceptable to many Christians, must be investigated. Their insidious ability to deceive, however, is not readily apparent until their genesis, ascendency, and aftermath are examined. In short, a look at history will help define the present by uncovering the past for the purpose of shaping the future. Knowing how we arrived at our present juncture will clarify the issues and give the church the perspective to act wisely and courageously. Congregations, pastors, and musicians must have such understanding if church music is to fulfill its potential. Without discerning how major worldviews affect church music, music ministry cannot hope to accomplish its mission.

Notes

1. John P. Newport, *Biblical Philosophy and the Modern Mind* (Fort Worth: Southwestern Baptist Theological Seminary, 1968), 81.

2. Susan Sontag, *Against Interpretation*, (New York: Dell, 1961), 293–304.

3. *Circus* (June 30, 1981), pp. 21–22.

4. Andrew Fletcher, *Conversation Concerning a Right Regulation of Government for the Common Good of Mankind* (1703); quoted in Nat Shapiro, comp., *An Encyclopedia of Quotations About Music* (New York: Da Capo, 1977), 235.

5. George Gerbner quoted in William F. Fore, *Image and Impact* (New York: Friendship, 1970), 8.

6. *U. S. News and World Report* (October 28, 1985), 46.

7. William M. Brailsford, "Ex Humanitas Veritas," *Genesis* 2 (April–May 1988): 10.

8. Robert Pattison, *The Triumph of Vulgarity* (New York: Oxford University, 1987), 9.

9. Ibid., v–xii, 12–29.

10. Dan Peters and Steve Peters, *Why Knock Rock?* (Minneapolis: Bethany House, 1984), 105.

11. Ibid., 105.

12. Ibid., 106.

13. Ibid., 107.

14. Pattison, *Triumph*, 120.

15. Interview with Bob Martinez, governor of Florida, "Should Dirty Lyrics Be Against the Law?," *U.S. News and World Report*, 25 June 1990, 24.

16. Allan Bloom, *The Closing of the American Mind* (New York: Simon and Schuster, 1987), 73.

17. Pattison, *Triumph*, 108.

18. Ibid., 111.

19. David A. Noebel, *Rock 'N' Roll: A Prerevolutionary Form of Cultural Subversion* (Tulsa: American Christian College, n.d.), 10.

20. Ibid., 3.

21. H. R. Rookmaaker, *Modern Art and the Death of a Culture* (Downers Grove, Ill.: InterVarsity, 1970), 188.

22. Ibid., 190.

23. Miriam Horn in a conversation with Isaac Stern, "Enchanting Your Child With Music," *U.S. News and World Report*, 13 August 1990, 67.

24. Isaiah 1–5; Jeremiah 1–11; Malachi 1–4.

25. 2 Peter 1–2; 1 John 2:15; Ephesians 6:12; Romans 12:2.

26. Will Herberg, "What Is the Moral Crisis of Our Time?" *Intercollegiate Review* 22 (Fall 1986): 9.

27. Bloom, *Closing*.

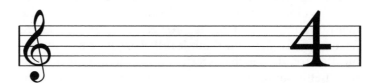

History: Setting Out the Problem

All human activity is shaped by the presuppositions of individuals and nations. Taken together, these presuppositions form what is called a worldview and are concerned with everything we are and do. Our understanding of and attitude toward God, history, humanity, morality, the universe, and death are all included. A worldview is a viewpoint, an orientation around which we live that gives meaning to existence. At its most elemental stage, it is concerned with questions of self and one's relationship to the world. At a more mature level, questions of ultimate reality are broached.

Everyone has a worldview. We cannot get around it. Our assumptions may be conscious or unconscious, carefully conceived or casually assumed personal convictions or societal mores. But they will be there. Even those who emphatically deny having a philosophy of life or worldview, are immediately admitting to a philosophy—that of not having one. In itself, this becomes a philosophical basis which will determine their general life orientation.

Major Worldviews

Art forms are shaped by their creator's worldview. Changing types and styles of church music usually reflect both the times in which they were written and the individual philosophical assumptions of each composer. Therefore it would be well to define briefly the major views and philosophies which have influenced church composition. It must be noted that these views are not one-dimensional. Some philosophical changes have resulted in the betterment of human society. Yet the overall trend has been away from a sound biblical theism. As a way of underscoring this trend, the characterization of the plight of human culture below may seem to be incomplete and one-sided. It is. For the sake of clarity, only those presuppositions fundamentally germane to the developments which have led to prevailing twentieth-century church music practice have been included.

Christian Theism

Christian theism is the worldview of the redeemed. God is the central proposition: he created the world, remains personally involved in it, and has endowed it with meaning. Though God made men and women is his own image, they fell into sin. The breach, however, can be healed by acceptance of Christ's atoning work. Death is the gate into everlasting life with our Lord. History is a linear stream of events over which God is sovereign. Right living is based on God's character, and his will is revealed in Jesus and the written Word. With God as the ultimate authority, life revolves around him.

Deism

Deism subtly shifted the tenets of theism. In order to justify humanity's taking a more elevated place in the world, God's involvement (immanence) was discounted. He was like a cosmic watchmaker, who, after making the watch (the universe), left it to run on its own. Though God exists, he is no longer active in human affairs. Consequently, human reason becomes all-important and replaces special revelation (the Bible). The rationality of the universe is thought to justify the belief that truth comes not through divine revelation but through human knowledge and right thinking. God can be seen in what he has made (general revelation) though he is personally irrelevant to it.

Naturalism

Naturalism does away with the existence of God. The human race is but an accident of "eternal" matter. As material mechanisms, people are sovereign in every respect. At death they become extinct. Naturalists feel some obligation to embrace a code of values, but these are not given by God as in theism or deduced from the natural world as in deism. People must invent their own individual value systems.

Nihilism

Nihilism is a reverse type of philosophy since it denies the possibility of purpose, value, knowledge, ethics, aesthetics, morality, and anything else of value, real or metaphysical, Nihilism absolutely repudiates any basis for meaning. It is emptiness. A logical outcome of naturalism's lack of adequate reasons as to why a person/machine should act responsibly, nihilism ends in chaos, anarchy, and despair. The only logic is absurdity. Everything is nothing.

Existentialism

Existentialism aims to help men and women rise from the ashes of nihilism to find within themselves some semblance of purpose and meaning. If nihilism reduced people to an insignificant roll of the dice, existentialism resurrects them to be the significant roller of the dice. This perspective seeks to authenticate existence by accepting whatever exists and by creating meaning subjectively. Dismissing history as inconsequential and untrustworthy, existentialism places emphasis on the here and now with people as the arbiter and perpetuator of that which is important, meaningful, and true "for me." An important commonality between the various branches of existentialism is the subjectivity which clearly raises the individual above anything else. Though other people, universal values, and great truths are "out there," what is important is only that which works for the individual person. "I" am the sole judge of significant meaning. There is no absolute truth or objective right and wrong except as I determine them applicable to me. Essentially, I do what I feel like doing.

New Age

Among the many other worldviews which could be mentioned, one is particularly noteworthy because of its growing popularity. Variously named New Age, New Wave, or New Consciousness, this viewpoint is particularly difficult to pin down. Despite variations in presuppositions, they all have two things in common: first, utter contempt for a single supernatural God who breaks in upon humanity with an authoritative Word; and, second, preoccupation with the self. New Ageism is a significant philosophical movement (with its own music!). Its chameleon-like adaptability promises to make it one of many worldviews vying for the allegiance of people for years to come.[1]

Homogenization

These worldviews are not as neatly defined and packaged as they appear to be. There are mutations, alterations, and variations, with many borrowings and much intermixing. Rarely does one find a true nihilist (actually it would be impossible to live as an out and out nihilist) or naturalist. The usual approach is for a person's worldview to be an amalgamation of many things. The process of defining a specific worldview is really the process of distilling individual assumptions.

Many worldviews with various adaptations exist simultaneously within any given culture. Because a worldview is a personal thing, each individual and group is bound to have a somewhat different way of apprehending reality. Therefore the value systems of an egalitarian society such as our own vary tremendously. Such pluralism is one of the special characteristics which has marked the culture of the twentieth century.

Nevertheless, simultaneously existing worldviews are influenced by a dominant view in any given culture and time. It is important to note that the culture of every historical period had certain philosophical assumptions, general attitudes, and a feeling tone which tended to dominate that culture. Dominant and overarching cultural characteristics tend to modify concurrent worldviews in varying degrees. For example, it is entirely possible, even probable, to find theism subtly changed because of an accommodation to the spirit of a particular age. In this way each worldview may be altered ever so subtly and unconsciously.

Historical Periods

History is a linear stream of events without clear demarcation between one historical period and another. The old and the new co-exist in a kind of ongoing cultural evolution. When specific characteristics in a given space of time become predominant, we often assign the era a name appropriate to its dominant motif. Distinguishing the preeminent assumptions aids us in marking the general drift and direction of a culture.

The church's music has been affected in every age by the prevailing worldview or spirit of that age. As we have previously noted, our concern here is for the main philosophical trends which have acted upon cultures to bring church music to its present state. Such an examination will deal with the most important issues, those with the broadest scope.

The Medieval Church

Beginning as a despised and persecuted minority, the early church grew in strength and maturity. Its zealous evangelism advanced Christianity to a place of supreme importance and authority. During the Middle Ages (c. 500–1450) the church enjoyed prominence in nearly all earthly and heavenly matters.

On occasion, temporal concerns outweighed spiritual ones; the spiritual became a cloak for the real goal of acquiring yet more power and wealth. Some clergy came to be treated as princes; the laity often pawns in their hands. So powerful did the church become that by the end of the Middle Ages it owned approximately 33% of Europe's land,[2] exercising its authority in ways which were sometimes contrary to its central mission. The church contained within itself sure evidence of its adamic frailty.

However, a societal atmosphere of God consciousness existed in the Middle Ages that has never been equalled. This was largely due to the tremendous presence and influence of the church. Kingdoms, municipalities, states, and governments changed again and again. But the church stayed. It was the glue which held society together, the foundation stone upon which everything was built.

The Middle Ages was a time when heavenly life received greater emphasis than earthly life. Strong belief in life after death was one of the common assumptions which unified existence. The few short years on earth were but preparation for the life to come. In the whole scheme of things ultimate destiny ranked far above earthly ease and comfort.

The medieval mind endowed the most common things with religious significance. God was invoked in all matters tem-

poral and religious. There were no "sacred" and "secular" categories. Art, music, and drama had but one end—the praise of
God. No cost was too much, no effort too great to bring to pass
that which brought glory to the Creator. Hence, art was full of
ecclesiastical symbolism. In music, triple meter had religious
significance because it was thought to symbolize the three per-
sons of the Trinity. The musical interval of an augmented fourth
was avoided because its lack of consonance was thought to
represent the *diabolus in musica*, the devil in music.

The monastic movement began as a means of protecting
the faith from pagan influence, of preserving scholarship and
learning, as a means of guarding the scriptures and developing
spiritual discipline. Religious orders also kept alive the arts,
laboriously making copy after copy of the scriptures, church
liturgies, and chant books. The monasteries provided civil as well
as spiritual continuity throughout the turbulence of the Middle
Ages. Though not perfect, monks modeled Christian behavior
through charitable deeds and spiritual witness. In large measure
it was the church's monastic orders which not only preserved
civilization but kept alive the church's true mission in the world,
the making of disciples.

The medieval spirit was one of godly mysticism and
otherworldliness. God gave life, nourished it, and received it
back at death. The preoccupation with the divine shows the
decidedly theistic orientation of the Middle Ages. God, the God
of the universe, the infinite, omniscient, omnipresent, omnipo-
tent One who rules over the affairs of humankind, is absolutely
supreme. People lived to serve him with their work and worship.

Though battered by pagan influences, society remained
church-oriented and God-fearing. In periods of expansionism or
revisionism the church endured. Medieval theistic culture sur-
vived everything except one thing and that was people.

The Renaissance

The momentum which had been building in the later
Middle Ages to elevate people to a more prominent position in
the scheme of things eventually changed medieval theocentric
orientation to the anthropocentrism of a new age, the Renaissance. It is impossible to find one specific cause or single event
for the shift which can be used to precisely date its beginning. In
one sense the Renaissance had its antecedents in the Garden of

Eden with Adam and Eve's preoccupation with their own ego-centricity. But in the more restrictive sense the years 1400–1600 are generally held to be the years in which humanity came into its own. Traditional medieval concerns of religion and faith were gradually discarded for more human concerns. Pleasure did not have quite the stigma attached to it that it formerly had when self-denial was the order of the day. The world exploded in an impetuous dynamic of discovery, creativity, and experimentation. Politics, economics, science, art, music, and philosophy were all beneficiaries of increased attention. Printing, gun powder, and geographic exploration gave humans increased communication, power, and vision. Studies in astronomy, medicine, and mathematics widened understanding of the natural world. People began to shake off the yoke of the church's absolute authority, leading to their questioning of all authority. The unrelenting march toward total human freedom was on.

The word *renaissance* literally means rebirth. Though specifically referring to a rebirth of classical learning, the term later developed a much broader and more inclusive meaning. The Renaissance was the turning point of Western civilization.

The overall attitude of the Renaissance repudiated the otherworldliness of medieval culture. This manifested itself in self-centeredness, self-determination, self-assertion, self-pleasure, self-awareness, self-actualization, self-assurance, self-acceptance, self-cultivation, self-interest, self-esteem, and self-importance. Humanity was feted, celebrated, and honored. Though given dignity by the Creator, men and women had their own dignity, abilities, and rewards. A preoccupation with worldly pursuits edged them ever closer to secularism.

It is precisely this changing of focus from divinity to humanity which gives us the name which most clearly sums up Renaissance philosophy and practice: humanism. Unfortunately, it has become a "buzzword" for many people, a catch-all term. It is used for differing philosophic emphases, all of which are connected by their concern for the human, but which are often substantially different from one another. Not only do we have humanism categorized by country (such as the Italian, French, or English Renaissance), but by content: Renaissance humanism, naturalistic humanism, atheistic humanism, modern humanism, twentieth-century humanism, religious humanism, and secular humanism.

At its core, humanism asserts the dignity and worth of the individual, an assumption quite in keeping with a theistic worldview. Made in the image of God, people do have worth. Yet at once we can see the problem: Renaissance humanism taken to extreme results in but one thing—the idolatry of self.

As Christians we must acknowledge that the Renaissance, with its attendant humanism, gave impetus to taking seriously the creation mandate. The awareness that we must fulfill our God-given responsibility to develop the potential of our world is indebted to those centuries long ago when people first took seriously the developing of their own gifts.

But we must also recognize that the direction in which the Renaissance set culture's path was potentially dangerous. The unshakable faith we presently have in humankind's ability to solve its own problems and to infuse life with purpose and meaning is a legacy of Renaissance humanism. This is not to fault the Renaissance per se. But the adaptations of Renaissance philosophy have the capacity for taking us far afield from God-centered living.

Interestingly, the Protestant Reformation and the Catholic Counter Reformation were actually counterparts to the Renaissance. That is, they were not phenomena spawned by the Renaissance spirit as much as they were conservative forces flowing from the Middle Ages which tended to mitigate the more extreme humanistic advances of the Renaissance. Their purposes were to strengthen faith, not to dismantle it. Amid evidences of the move away from medieval Christianity, the reformers did everything in their power to establish the normalcy of the centrality of the Christian faith in human life. Indeed, it was Luther's specific intention to "rekindle this spirit, this most valuable inheritance of the Middle Ages, and so to make it fruitful for the future history of Western civilization."[3] The reform movements tended to slow down society's discarding of the spiritual in favor of the temporal.

Once the Renaissance was in motion, it generated increasing change. One can find, however, trends which reached back, or pulled back from the tendencies which later ushered in a post-Christian age. Humanism did not advance in equally graduated steps.

The Age of Reason

The seventeenth and eighteenth centuries have been termed the Age of Reason and were marked by a buoyant optimism. The individual, in cooperation with nature (which, as mechanism, could be logically understood and used), believed that through human reason nothing was impossible. Though God was acknowledged, deism (the determinative worldview of the time) ruled him irrelevant. Unlocking the secrets of God's natural world ranked as the chief priority, the key to satisfying the self-conscious quest for power that had arisen in every field of endeavor.

Although the "Age of Reason" is generally applied to a two hundred-year period, the eighteenth century deserves special treatment. Termed the "Enlightenment," it was a time of increased dependence on human reason. Rationality bypassed revelation as the guide to behavior; faith was suspect. The general assumptions of the Middle Ages were rejected firmly, vehemently, even passionately. Faith in reason replaced Christian doctrine; the unity of the sacred and secular was shattered. Intellectuals resented the authority of the church. Answers to life's problems appeared to lie not in heaven, but on earth. Political, social, intellectual, economic, artistic, and spiritual freedom surpassed faith and dependence in God in importance. Humankind was ready at last to leave the nest. People could take care of themselves.

The belief that humanity may control the world was revolutionary. It was truly seen as an enlightenment. The abolishing of the historic position God had in the affairs of the world was one of the Enlightenment's lasting legacies; another was its turning a more balanced Renaissance humanism into a more humanistic one. The dignity of humankind in the Renaissance turned to the sovereignty of the individual in the Enlightenment. Self-sufficient rationalism encouraged people not only to understand nature, but to manipulate it for their own ends. Reason, properly applied, seemed quite sufficient.

Such deistic thought lead directly to naturalism. The realization came that if God is really irrelevant and unnecessary to human life, then perhaps he has only been an imaginary figure all along. Eventually the deistic view of God gave way to the naturalist's belief that God does not exist at all.

Naturalism, the product of the Enlightenment, became tremendously significant in establishing human autonomy. Developing in the nineteenth and twentieth centuries, it become one of the most persistent and influential worldviews of the last three centuries.[4]

Romanticism

The drift to human autonomy was completed in the nineteenth century. With the theory of evolution postulated by Charles Darwin and with society's continuing technological and scientific progress, it seemed that men and women had control of the earth; people were secure, self-reliant, even invincible.

With such an exalted position, many believed themselves obligated to no higher authority. But without a higher law, human objectivity fails. Individuality, subjectivity, and personal opinion became the modes of apprehending reality. Yet, if reality is really a matter of individual interpretation can there be universal truth, logic, and reason at all?

It is in just this dilemma that the nineteenth-century romanticists found themselves embroiled. Reason failed; objectivity was a myth. Facts alone were sterile and cold. Without personal interpretation they were ultimately useless. The only answer is for "me" to focus on reality as "I" see it. Without restraints of any kind, giving free reign to one's impulses liberates the self so that "my" truth can be found.

Of course, according so much weight to subjectivity led to a kind of idealized escapism in which the world was seen as the individual wanted to see it—a subjective haze we call romanticism. Since there is no "law" everything is a matter of personal taste. Romanticism meant individualism, and this led to unrestrained license. The pendulum swung from reason to emotion. Feeling, not the logic of argument, carried the day. Truth was something felt, not something intellectually known. Rules, order, and law were anathema. Classical ideals were replaced by individual passion and personalized expression without bounds. The rational world could not contain the romantics. They longed for something better—another world, a fantasy world which could never be. Romanticism fell in love with a narcissistic dream.

The Twentieth Century

Not surprisingly, many of the philosophic assumptions of the twentieth century are but the flowering of earlier presuppositions. Romanticism in the arts continued, often pushing personal expression to a brash if not brutal vulgarity. Naturalism turned to nihilism, a stasis of nothingness in which despair, suicide, anarchy, and absurdity were common themes. Found not only in works of art and the writings of philosophers, they were obvious in the world at large: two world wars, genocide, nuclear bombs, suicide, torture, indiscriminate killing, and a frantic search for pleasurable fulfillment. Existentialism, with its emphasis on the need for individual authentication of life through rebellion and action, attempted to rescue society from outmoded philosophical systems or those believed untenable. The New Age movement continued to gain momentum as men and women sought for answers to life's questions. All in all it was a tremendously eclectic age.

The Spirit of Our Age

Individualism

Individualism, reaching new heights of importance, became the underlying trait of contemporary culture. "In my view," or "my opinion is," or "I believe that," or "I feel that," are expressions that frequently exhibit that individualism. We have come to assume that reality is merely a "viewpoint" apprehended subjectively. Nothing is true unless it is true "for me." Such an orientation disavows objectivity and authority. Moral, ethical, theological, and aesthetic absolutes are discarded. Only authority over which there is no choice (such as civil government) is tolerated.

Relativism

Relativism is another common trait which has become entwined in contemporary life. Because it is well established it is very difficult to perceive. The twentieth century's penchant for pluralism of every kind has made it unacceptable to believe in something to the exclusion of something else.

This philosophy espouses the absolute equality of everything. All values and value systems, regardless of their conflicting perspectives, are equally valid. Right and wrong are reduced to mere opinion, one is as good as the other. Truth is not fixed but changeable, relative to the whims which define it. The most we can say about relativism is that there is no way to define its parameters, since anything goes.

Relativism produces a culture which is insipid in its moral, aesthetic, ethical, and philosophical judgments. Excessive concern to avoid intolerance leads to a normless society. There can be no clear consensus on issues because truth lacks the anchor of what D. Elton Trueblood calls an "objective reference." "Why shouldn't the slave owner reply to Woolman's approach by the answer, 'I like it that way?' What was to keep Hitler from claiming that persecution of the Jews was *his* truth?"[5] In making truth mere viewpoint, relativism sets the table for a feast of self-indulgent autonomy.

Materialism

We have become a consumer-oriented society. Our desire to get is exceeded only by our desire to get more. Shopping is now a national pastime. One of the advertising industry's main tasks is to create product demand as well as to give out product information. The methods employed are often as questionable as the suppositions from which they proceed. The push to sell, regardless of need or the buyer's financial resources, is the big challenge. In a climate where the accumulation of material possessions is a way of life, the term merchandising takes on new meaning.

Hedonism

The hedonistic drive (pleasure is the highest good) of the twentieth century is well known, simply one more indication that the spirit of our age is to be found in satisfying the self. Yielding to the insatiable appetite of the adamic nature has caused a frenzy of pleasure-seeking. Whether it be "innocent" pastime or foul lewdness, contemporary men and women largely live to pleasure themselves.

Entertainment is one significant way that our culture gratifies the hedonistic urge. The pursuit of amusement, leisure, and fun has skewed our value system so that teachers, for example, who shape the very destiny of our young, are paid vastly less than ball players, movie actors, and rock stars, who routinely are paid millions. Dollars go where values are; we live as though amusement is more valuable than knowledge!

Amoralism—Defining a New Culture

The most telling characteristic of our culture is the lack of an absolute moral reference. Today there is widespread acceptance that there is no God-given morally binding law to break. Hence sin, which is the breaking of God's law, does not exist. People are free to do whatever they wish without accountability and without guilt. Men and women, on their own recognizance, do what they want since there are no absolutes to hold them back.

Contemporary culture is radically different from any we have previously examined. Its conglomerate center has retained only a shattered vestige of an integrated theistic worldview. That is, it is not only acceptable but normal to live without regard for biblical absolutes, a change so sweeping that we have only begun to ascertain its effects. Such a revolution influences everything, including music. Though many are blind to it, the amoralism of society is a fact of contemporary life.

The Big "I" Equals Immaturity

We are presently reaping the consequences of society's anthropocentric stance: selfism, pure and unadorned. By usurping the place of God, people have returned to the egocentricity of the Fall. Turned out of the garden, they have made themselves a quagmire.

That quagmire is the immaturity of self-centered existence. Such immaturity can be made to sound so sophisticated, so psychologically and intellectually satisfying, that its essential quality is masked. Nevertheless, in the end, selfism boils down to nothing but the immaturity of infantilism!

The big "I" is the problem. The movement of Western civilization in the last six hundred years has been toward the enthronement of the individual, and the end is not in sight. No doubt there will be variation upon variation of its basic orientation—ever new developments in the autonomy of men and women. The problem will not go away, and the contemporary church cannot escape it.

Notes

1. Douglas Groothuis, *Confronting the New Age* (Downers Grove, Ill.: InterVarsity, 1988), 32.

2. Will Durant, *The Story of Philosophy* (New York: Washington Square, Inc., 1968), 104, quoting J. H. Robinson and C. Beard, *Outlines of European History* (Boston: 1914, n.p.) i., 443.

3. Gerhard Ritter, *Luther: His Life and Work* (New York: Harper & Row, 1963), 213.

4. James Sire, *The Universe Next Door* (Downers Grove, Ill.: InterVarsity, 1987), 82–83.

5. D. Elton Trueblood, "Intellectual Integrity," *Faculty Dialogue* 7 (Winter 1984–85): 47.

Humanistic Trends in Worship and Music

Tracing the history of Western worldviews gives us a clear picture of culture's steady drift toward human autonomy. That move, unrelenting in its press for influence and control, has deeply affected the Christian church. Evangelism, teaching, and worship, as well as daily Christian living, have all been changed, albeit subtly, by the humanistic influence to make individuals and their desires supreme. Church music has been part of that change. Since worship is the primary place where church music occurs, this activity will be examined in some detail. We will investigate the impact that extreme humanistic tendencies of culture have had on worship music, and, in subsequent chapters, we will suggest ways to counteract them.

Worship and Selfism

Worship

Congregations, pastors, and musicians ought be tremendously concerned for the quality of the church's worship. It is true that worship will continue as long as the church meets.

Come what may, the community of believers will not forgo the assembling of the faithful. But, like anything else in the economy of God, good, better, and best worship are possible. Just because the church gathers does not mean that all is well within its walls.

Worship is conditioned culturally because we worship through cultural forms. When these cultural forms are in contention with and in contrast to theistic principles, something has to give. If such alien forms are used in worship (in the attempt to accommodate the gospel to culture, for example), they change the gospel. It would be better to stand up to culture and reassert the validity of the church's standards, thereby risking a limited separation from the world. The church must not assume a stance of unqualified acceptance of culture.

Frankly, it is revealing—even shocking—to discover the extent of the world's influence on the actual shape and content of church worship. Many church groups, even those who like to feel themselves "in the world but not of the world" would be surprised at the inroads culture has made into their most revered worship practices. The only thing that will save the church from a distorted worship is a clear understanding of the problem and the will to act accordingly.

Some cultural manifestations are clearly seen for what they are and are dealt with in a more or less straightforward manner. The absence of moral absolutes, for example, has not gone unnoticed by most church bodies. But other areas of cultural accommodation are not so easy to spot. For this reason they may be even more damaging than those which are readily perceived as blatantly wrong.

Aesthetics and Theism

One such area, aesthetics, is the most immediately concerned with music. All worldviews include assumptions which shape the arts. Remarkably, church music's aesthetic presuppositions often come more from culture's non-theistic norms than from theistic ones! This results in a warped and fragmented Christian worldview.

Christians have been influenced by the general culture into believing that there are no divine imperatives, no aesthetic absolutes or standards. We have believed aesthetics to be a matter of personal taste, a matter of subjective discrimination:[1] "I like green, you like blue—so what? One is as good as the other. There is no right or wrong." Our faith is not applied consistently to all of life. As Christians we find ourselves becoming compartmentalized with theistic standards for some things and selfistic standards for others. Indeed,

> one of the great inconsistencies of many evangelical Christians is the schizophrenia between insistence on objectivity of Christian values in ethics and the parallel belief of complete subjectivity in aesthetics. The same preacher who believes that he is obligated to preach objective righteousness in morality often implies that "anything goes" in the music of the church. This is one area where naturalistic humanists find, perhaps with good reason, a wide crack in the Christian door.[2]

Music has become but a matter of personal preference. In becoming aesthetic subjectivists, Christians have moved toward a naturalistic, existentialist, or secular humanistic philosophy, allowing individuals to become their own authority.

Theists must be objectivists through and through. God is the authority. He sets the standard. In worship God's objective aesthetic norms, derived from both special and general revelation, ought be adhered to. To believe that God has remained silent on artistic matters is to misunderstand completely the nature and scope of revelation. All worthy art is based on God-given aesthetic principles that are laid down in creation and are cross-cultural and timeless. As the consummate artist, God and his standards are the objective criteria by which all art is judged.[3]

Nowhere is our penchant for subjectivity better seen than in the aesthetic understanding of young people. It is most telling to watch the faces of college students the first time they become aware that aesthetic evaluation might be more than a matter of taste. All kinds of reactions are visible: indifference, curiosity, shock, even anger that their personal tastes could be called into question. Subjectivity is so firmly entrenched as their way of apprehending the world that judging the objective merits of art, music, or drama is not even an operative possibility. To state that J. S. Bach's music is better than the music of Prince stretches their incredulity to the limit. Beauty, it is said, is totally in the eye of the beholder!

Church music needs an aesthetic, a church music theology if you will, that comes from the Word of God. The great doctrines of creation, the *imago Dei*, the incarnation, stewardship, and eschatology have much to say about music in the church.[4] If we let our subjective desires run away with the church's music, we have denied the very nature of that which we believe. Allowing the Word of God its say in our music-making assures us that it will be a manifestation of God's word to us.

Subjectivism in Church Music's Texts

The aesthetic subjectivism of culture can also be found in the words of Christian songs. Selfism, culture's humanistic mind-set, plainly reveals itself in many of our texts. The focus on "me" is most problematical; the church is supposed to be a corporate entity with God as the focus of attention! "Wounded for Me," a two-line, five-stanza hymn, uses the personal pronoun an incredible twenty-eight times![5] Technically it may be about Jesus, but practically the central focus of the song is clearly the individual.

The increasing momentum of Renaissance humanism can be seen in the church's hymnody. Most Latin hymnody (AD 300–1400), for example, is objective. God is the subject. But during the seventeenth and eighteenth centuries the humanistic tendencies begun in the Renaissance became more prominent. Theists, influenced by a worldview which increased humankind's importance and decreased God's, wrote extremely introspective texts. During the Romantic era they became even more syrupy and sentimental.

The gospel song movement in the nineteenth century gave new meaning to the concept of religious self-interest. Songs such as "Will There Be Any Stars in My Crown?"[6] and "A Sinner Like Me!"[7] were typical of the "me-centrism" of culture's progress. Coupled with a melodramatic nostalgia, they joined the trend toward complete subjectivity. Gospel songs such as "My Mother's Prayer," ("As I wandered 'round the homestead, Many a dear familiar spot Bro't within my recollection Scenes I'd seemingly forgot"),[8] as well as "I Am Coming, Dear Saviour,"[9] were typical of the genre's selfistic orientation.

Christian music in the twentieth century has continued in the same direction. The spirit of the age relentlessly stresses self-centered concerns. A survey of Contemporary Christian Music (CCM), the most popular genre of religious music, shows many songs transparently, even heretically, oriented around the satisfaction of people. "We Get Lifted Up"[10] is an example. It begins: "I've learned a little secret that you may already know." That secret turns out to be that praising the Lord "does as much for us as it does for Him 'Cause we get lifted up!" The refrain then continues in the same vein: "We get lifted up, we get lifted up, we get lifted up when we praise the Lord; Oh, we get lifted up, we get lifted up, we get lifted up when we praise the Lord." The second stanza opens, "I used to think my praise was only meant to serve the King." But now we realize that praising Jesus "does as much for us as it does for Him." The refrain is then repeated, highlighting the emphasis and focus of the song. Yes, we do get lifted up when we worship; but when our preoccupation is with the self (getting lifted up), as it is in this song, then worship is convoluted, reflecting culture's elevation of people over God. A sampling of new publications indicates that production of such material continues unabated. We like to sing about ourselves. Church music and church musicians are in the mainstream of the privatization of religion.

Pleasuring the Self

Congregations in our subjective and humanistic culture want music which "speaks to me." What exactly does that mean? A consideration of the pleasure syndrome is helpful here. Though Christians are liable to repudiate the suggestion that many people worship for pleasure, or confuse pleasure and worship, a case can be made to show the conflict between principle and practice. The hedonistic bent of our culture can be found in the church's worship practices.

The plea for music "which speaks to me" is a rather telling phrase. It is first an indication of the importance we place upon self. The demand that "number one" be satisfied is extraordinarily indicative of the real priority that many Christians (no matter what they claim) place on themselves. A selfish orientation is not readily seen as contradictory to the very nature of the Christian faith. Second, the phrase in question, "music which speaks to me," simply means, practically speaking, "music which I like." Musical pleasure, "my" musical pleasure, becomes the criterion by which the church's music is judged.

Religious terminology often masks the out-and-out honesty of simply saying, "We will respond only to what we like."

Instead, we say that the criterion for church music is that it "bless me," "move me," "minister to me," or "bring me closer to God." Such statements camouflage the real criterion by which we judge music's success—pleasure. Hedonists within the church believe that liking something is *the* prerequisite for its effectiveness in ministering. Seldom do parishioners tell musicians, "I disliked the music today, but it helped me grow in Christ." We are so attuned to amusement that worship music must pleasure us—or else. The hard sayings of Jesus, such as, "If any man will come after me, let him deny himself, and take up his cross daily, and follow me"[11] are seldom translated into "hard" musical sayings.

Phrases such as, "I enjoyed the music," or, "I loved that song," or "the special music was thrilling" point up the fact that the way we value something is largely by how much we like it. The expression, "that really ministered to me," is in general, a statement about the emotional disposition engendered in the listener by his or her pleasurable response. Lamentably, enjoyment then becomes the basis for ministerial worth since any other standard is believed unimportant. No matter what is said, most Christians prefer amusement to discipline.

Individualistic self-indulgence is displayed often by disgruntled parishioners who believe that they are not being "fed" in worship. Worship exists, they argue, "to feed me"—meaning "to please me." The pleasure they get out of worship becomes the test of its validity. However, the worshiper who is always calculating what he or she is "getting out" of the service is missing the whole point of worship: worship is not introverted. It is extroverted—we give to God as we celebrate *his* acts. That is the essence of worship. When personal gratification is worship's objective, worship is invalidated. To leave the service with the query, "Now what did I get out of church today?" is to misunderstand the nature of worship. Such worshipers define it by their own pleasurable self-satisfaction, another way of saying that hedonism is not all that secular.

Popular Music in Church

When the main criterion for choosing the music used in worship is pleasure, then the music specifically crafted for that purpose becomes the logical choice. In our culture that means the music of pop, with its melody, rhythm, and harmony having but one goal, easy self-gratification. Whether it be rock 'n' roll, rock, country, CCM, heavy metal, new wave, gospel, country rock, swing, or rap, pop is the preferred music of most people.

Enthusiasm for pop music, especially rock, has had devastating results. Its popularity has not gone unnoticed by church musicians; accordingly, they have responded by using more and more music based on popular models. As the wider culture has grown increasingly preoccupied with the drive to fulfill personal pleasurable desires, the church has been there supplying a religious counterpart. The latest development, CCM, (much of which utilizes stylistic traits based on rock and whose texts are often humanistically self-centered), crowds out more mature musical expressions. Church leaders, not the least of whom have been the musicians, have naively attempted to compete with rock's popularity on its own ground—only to offer a twisted and mangled theism in the place of the full gospel.

> Rock knocks the props out from under religion, first, by shifting the locus of faith from God to self, and secondly, by depriving sects and churches of their claim to exclusive revelation. By forcing churches to compete on the basis of their ability to titillate the instincts of their worshippers, vulgar pantheism [rock] compels the champions of organized religions to abandon their pretension to superior truth and turns them into entrepreneurs of emotional stimulation. Once God becomes a commodity used for self-gratification, his fortunes depend on the vagaries of the emotional marketplace, and his claim to command allegiance on the basis of omnipotence or omniscience vanishes in a blaze of solipsism as his priests and shamans pander to the feeling, not the faith, of their customers.[12]

The result of using religious rock in worship is dangerous: The church service becomes a make-believe fantasy-world used to satisfy the less noble traits of the adamic nature.

Immaturity—The Result of Pop

Religious pop music contributes to spiritual immaturity. Its musical and textual ethos subverts one of the church's basic tasks: helping people to grow up in Christ. Pop is not a mature music, but merely an easy-come, easy-go type of immediate musical gratification. To turn it into a medium for Christian growth is naive at best and destructive at worst. This is not to say that gospel artists, Christian contemporary musicians, or choir directors who perform this music are insincere. But the individual Christian and the church as a whole are spiritually weakened when their musical expressions are based on the shifting sands of the pop genre. Pop, by whatever name, is hedonistic, and musical hedonism is not an adequate basis for building a strong spirituality. No matter how one might try, or what one believes, musical immaturity does not produce holistic Christian maturity.

The inroads of hedonism into church music can be seen in a variety of its expressions. Congregational songs, for example, often tend toward the simplistic, the trite, and the banal. Musical depth is avoided. This is especially true of the chorus singing made popular by certain segments of the church, parachurch organizations, and various renewal movements. While there is a proper place for it, chorus singing has encouraged many churches to ignore completely the hymnal. Becoming almost cultic in their disdain for musical and textual depth, they have opted instead for a playful, repetitive, easily memorizable chorus music that can be sung and danced to as if one were at a party. The following, sung a dozen or more times in succession, is but one example: "I've got a feeling everything's gonna be all right. I've got a feeling everything's gonna be all right. I've got a feeling everything's gonna be all right, all right, all right, all right." Not only is such a chorus trite, thereby making Christianity superficial, but it is also heretical. First, the song focuses exclusively on the individual. Second, feeling is the frame of reference. In worship, however, God ought be central. Moreover, faith, not feeling, should be the Christian's operative frame of reference. A faith practiced on the basis of feeling is no faith at all. Such songs may be fun to sing and make us feel good, but their effect on worship and life is devastating.

Choices for choir anthems are also being influenced. Music departments in many religious bookstores sell nothing but contemporary gospel hits. A recent informal survey of several of the more traditional music stores indicated that an increasing percentage of their choral music sales (in some cases over seventy percent) were of the pop genre. An amazing fact!

Church solo literature has also changed. Not only is Contemporary Christian Music the most popular type of this material, but its performance has been influenced by the technology common to pop. Sounds bigger than life are the norm. Congregations have come to expect the amplified decibel level of rock. Taped accompaniments of instrumental ensembles, always with a percussive beat, really catch the ear. The assembly becomes dissatisfied with less than the raucous sounds of a pop band or the luxurious novelty of a professionally produced studio orchestra. Daily listening to gospel pop creates an expectancy for more of the same on Sunday mornings. In actuality entertainment becomes the unacknowledged purpose of worship.

Entertainment in Worship

It is amusing to realize that our culture automatically assumes musicians to be entertainers. Secular job classifications are so arranged that musicians are routinely assigned the entertainment category. Certainly many musicians (especially those in the pop arts) think of themselves this way. It is an understandable assumption since most music is assimilated as entertainment.

The church musician too is commonly perceived as an entertainer, albeit a religious one. Unfortunately music ministry, no matter how religious we might believe it to be, has become to many a source of religious amusement. Not that this is admitted or that it is invariably so, but when the musician chooses music solely on the basis of its being liked by the congregation (emotionally fulfilling, devoid of reason, and in a pop style), then one can be sure that music ministry has become entertainment.

It is, literally, a grievous thought that worship music could serve such a purpose. While this is not the place to argue the validity of entertainment in general for the Christian, we do need to understand the pitfalls of allowing worship music to become an amusement.

Entertainment results when the backbone of musical reason is discarded in favor of musical emotionalism. That is to say, music which is cloying, sentimental, sweet, and uncreative amuses the listener. It is one-sided and too easily enjoyed, costing the listener little in the way of personal involvement in the art work. Entertainment music is not disciplined, and therefore, not a fitting symbolic representation of gospel meaning. It is purposely immature.

Amazingly pastors, congregations, and many church musicians have exhibited little recognition that religious pop music is entertainment. For instance, no matter how much we intend that CCM not be entertaining, it will be anyway. That is its nature. Secular musicians often have a better grasp than church musicians of how people react to music and of the appropriateness of certain types of music to accomplish particular ends. A nightclub musician plays dance music, easy listening music, music for losing control, or music for sense-deadening, depending on what is required at the moment. But church musicians have often been blind to the fact that church music's style must be guided by its function, and it must not be mixed with those styles which are easily confused with functions unrelated to worship.

In truth, most congregations simply want to follow the trends of their culture. They are afraid of being different, of being out of step. The indomitable self has determined that it must please itself and be entertained in giving praise to God. In nourishing musical immaturity in worship, the church retards spiritual growth.

Relativism is Contagious

One reason for so little concern about the type of music used in churches is that relativism has affected our church music value system. It is hard to conceive of a Christian knowingly offering to God something clearly perceived to be less than the best. That it happens is probably due not so much to a deliberate decision, but rather to a misunderstanding of the philosophical assumptions governing our judgments. The prevalent worldviews we have previously mentioned have prejudiced many Christians into believing that all music is of equal value; music A is as good as music B. If we reason that all music is qualitatively the same, the only basis left for choosing one music over another must then have to do with taste. This is a dangerous misunderstanding.

Aesthetic relativism contradicts the very theism upon which the church is founded. By choosing on the basis of fancy, we imply that standards do not exist. If that is so, why not regard ethics, morality, or stewardship in the same way? We are back into the relativist box once more. "I" can do what I want because there are no rules. Yet there are standards of excellence "that transcend both individual tastes and cultural norms";[13] to simply disavow such a claim does not invalidate it. Squelching aesthetic absolutes invariably exacts a high price—the establishment of an environment which encourages the breakup of a Christian value system.

The alarming thing about musical relativism is that it spreads like a cancer. Before one realizes it, the unity of the faith as it applies to life is broken. We either have to live dichotomized lives, consciously compartmentalizing one standard for this and another for that, or we must abandon standards altogether. It is a painful problem because the only way a relativist can be consistent is to ignore all absolutes. At that point we cease to be fully Christian.

Pragmatism in Worship

One of the manifestations of self-centeredness in worship is pragmatism. As a philosophy it repudiates absolute truth, allowing the self to determine truth by individual experience. Values flow from process.

To the pragmatist, process is not based upon principle; rather, results validate process. If it works, use it. Achieving predetermined ends justifies any means used to arrive at those goals. This methodology is unprincipled since the loss of an absolute center of reference gives license to doing whatever is necessary to achieve the objective. A pragmatist's only anchor is success at any cost.

One of pragmatism's weaknesses is its inability to discipline the methods used in reaching its goals. Pragmatists believe that methods are amoral, with little or no relationship to the ethical manner of how something is attained. No strong compulsion exists to judge the appropriateness of the means. The correctness of the method, according to the pragmatist, is determined solely by reaching the goal.

Christianity, however, is more procedure-oriented than goal-oriented. That is to say, our faith is not merely a set of beliefs isolated from right action. Genuine faith is dynamic, concerned with right action. Faith without good works is dead. Methods must be based upon biblical principles.

Background Music—Pragmatic Inducement

Many, if not most, church musicians and pastors tend to be pragmatists, and congregations tend to agree with this bent.

An example of such pragmatism is the use of background music to synthetically create atmosphere: preludes are required to get people "in the mood to worship," and background music gives to petitioners a certain feeling of devotional religiosity during prayers. When people are at the altar for receiving communion, in response to an invitation for conversion or for intercession, the organ is often called upon to provide "spiritual"; conditioning with its steady background halo of sound.

The stated goal for this seems good. We want our people to draw close to the Lord, feel his presence, and experience the warmth which we know comes from communion with the Almighty. We want a heartfelt worship, but giving mood music the job of achieving that goal is dangerous. Background music is a deadly trap. If we only realized what is taking place, there would be a quick change in the method used to achieve such noble goals.

Music has power, more power than we ordinarily assume. It is, in fact, one of the most powerful emotional mood makers available. Consider its usage on television and cinema for generating particular moods. One can almost predict a scene's content by the background music! It is this ability which has caught the fancy of church leaders.

The danger in using background music in worship is the human manufacture of religious feelings. Musically induced and manipulated atmosphere is a deception.

Leaders, without realizing it, use such music in place of the genuine working of the Spirit, and as worshipers we unconsciously accept it as the Spirit's work. But it is, nevertheless, a counterfeit. Background music generates the illusion of the Holy Spirit's work among the congregation because of its very real ability to generate emotional states. Moreover, the congregation becomes like Pavlov's dogs—dependent on outside stimulation for evidencing the response desired by the worship leader (the goalsetter). We become more and more dependent on musical background to "open us up to the Spirit." And when the stimulation is absent, we find we can no longer worship or open ourselves to the Spirit's working. Background music actually cripples us and promotes spiritual infantilism.

We should briefly note that God in his sovereignty is not limited by our attempts to produce results for him. That does not justify, however, the self-stimulative approach to worship. If God is sovereign, then leaders ought depend only on his sovereign work. Our job is to act rightly.

Human manipulation for divine ends is a contradiction in terms. For if we manipulate people into the kingdom, it is likely that someone else will be able to manipulate them out of the kingdom. If we allow divine ends to determine our means, then the sterling principles of God's economy will form the basis of our action. Pragmatism is then defeated. Real success in worship occurs when we leave the results to God.

Idolatry

Every manifestation of culture's collective worldview points to one thing—the aggrandizement of self. Subjectivism, hedonism, relativism, and pragmatism each have their center in the "I." The implications for worship stagger the imagination. Worship is the activity in which believers are supposed to empty themselves of self. Yet the archetypal sin of self (egocentricity and pride) is frequently present in much of our worship. Granted, it may be unconscious, but it is nevertheless dangerous. Worship that utilizes the subjective, hedonistic, pragmatic, and relativistic practices enumerated herein has its attention on the creature, not the Creator.

When the methods and materials shaping our worship are chosen on the basis of pleasing the worshiper, then we have broken the first commandment: "Thou shalt have no other gods before me." Worship which purposes to make people feel good is an activity whose purpose points back to them. Even though words might be given in praise of God, actions which selfishly point to private pleasure tell a different story. The individual idolatrously becomes the focus of worship.

Worship which uses music for pleasuring the assembly (music programmed on the basis of likability) results in making worshipers more immature because self-satisfaction becomes its purpose. Worship which ought to mature us in Christ then becomes a means of reinforcing our already ample self-centeredness.

It would be inaccurate to state categorically that worship practices always produce the same result in every worshiper. God, in his sovereignty and mercy, helps us in spite of our ineptitude. The point is that self-promoting music leads us in the wrong direction—the reversal of spiritual growth.

The centuries-long trend toward the enthronement of self has done much to invalidate our worship. We must address this problem if a sound biblical theism is to flourish in the twenty-first century. We cannot set ourselves up as gods and expect to worship Yahweh. Death to self (even in the musical realm) is necessary.

Notes

1. J. Brent Bill, *Rock and Roll* (Old Tappan, New Jersey: Fleming H. Revell Co., 1987), 22.

2. Dale A. Jorgenson, *Christianity and Humanism* (Joplin, Mo.: College Press, 1983), 49.

3. See Rookmaaker, *Modern Art*, 225–52.

4. See Calvin M. Johansson, *Music & Ministry: A Biblical Counterpoint* (Peabody, Mass.: Hendrickson, 1984).

5. W. G. Ovens (stanza one) and Gladys Westcott Roberts (stanzas two through five), "Wounded For Me," *Hymns of Glorious Praise* (Springfield, Mo.: Gospel Publishing House, 1969), 198.

6. E. E. Hewitt, "Will There Be Any Stars?," *Alexander's Gospel Songs*, comp.Charles M. Alexander (New York: Fleming H. Revell Company, 1908), 57.

7. C. J. Butler, "A Sinner Like Me!," *Gospel Hymns Nos. 1 to 6 Complete* (New York: Biglow & Main Co., 1894), 382.

8. T. C. O'Kane, "My Mother's Prayer," *Sacred Songs No. 1*, eds. Ira Sankey, James McGranahan, and George C. Stebbins (New York: Biglow and Main Co., 1896), 148.

9. H. N. Lincoln, "I Am Coming, Dear Saviour," *Songland Melodies*, (Dallas: Songland Company, 1897), 146.

10. Hal Spencer and Lynn Keesecker, "We Get Lifted Up," *Works of Heart* (Alexandria, Ind.: Alexandria House, 1984), 44.

11. Luke 9:23 (KJV).

12. Pattison, *Triumph*, 186.

13. Martin Gardner, *The Whys of a Philosophical Scrivener* (New York: William Morrow and Co., 1983), 67.

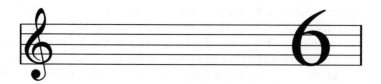

Discipline: The Road to Maturity

Must the church accept the anthropocentrism of culture? Does worship have to be structured on tenets contrary to its very nature? If the main purpose of music ministry is to promote holistic maturity in the believer, is it realistic to expect that goal to be achieved in an environment in which self has become a basic working principle? Further, after six hundred years of cultural and philosophical drift, can the church be expected to make any immediate and significant dent in culture's inroads?

These are difficult questions. To be in the world but not of it is perplexing. Yet as Christians we don't have to despair. There is hope. Open to God's guidance and willing to pay the price, we may steer a new course: one of faithfulness and integrity.

Discipleship

Discipline and Disciples

The way to maturity is discipline. The price we must pay, the corrective to self-idolization, is discipleship. Such discipline must be comprehensive: a discipleship of heart, mind, and soul; family, work, and worship; sermon, music, and prayer; hymn, chorus, and song; text, notes, and medium; harmony, melody, and rhythm. This will reorder the way we think, the way we live, and the way we worship.

Disciples are disciplined. It is their distinguishing mark. When disciplined in the ways of a master, disciples find their identity subjugated to the higher authority of their master. Christian disciples find themselves centered in God. He increases in us; we decrease. Laying ourselves at his feet and daily taking up our cross to follow him are required of every maturing Christian. Maturity means discipline.

Discipline, rightly understood and practiced, helps congregations, pastors, and musicians to achieve God's intent for his children. It usually brings to mind, however, tyrannical oppression, a stoic resolve to be serious, crabbedness, and a renunciation of fun. Not so. Christian discipline is a far cry from a casuistic legalism. Paradoxically, it is the Christian way to achieving personal freedom and fulfillment. But the emphasis must be on God, not on self. The renunciation of the latter frees us for a ministry disciplined by God and his Word rather than by pragmatic agendas or self-serving ends.

The ground of Christian discipline is humble (not legalistic) self-denial. Jesus' graphic example at the Last Supper is a poignant picture of humility, the model all disciples are to emulate. On his knees washing the disciples' feet, God, the Lord, the Creator, the Master, admonishes them to wash each others' feet: "For I have given you an example, that you also should do as I have done to you. Truly, truly, I say to you, a servant is not greater than his master; nor is he who is sent greater than he who sent him."[1] Obedient self-denial is the disciple's normal behavior.

Biblical Uses of the Word Discipline

The word discipline is used in several ways: restoration, equipping, correcting, and training. Each makes a significant contribution to the disciple's personal life and ministry. Church music composition, church music programs, and church musicians need to be disciplined and act as agents for discipling others.

The restoration sense of the word is used to make right that which has gone awry. In Mark 1:19 James and John are mending or "restoring" their nets. In 1 Corinthians 1:10, Paul admonishes the warring factions in the church to cease and desist their disunity and be "perfectly joined together" or "restored to one another" in the Lord Jesus Christ. In both instances we find that something has been torn or broken and that the action of restoring or discipling (*katartizein*) is needed to fix the problem. Discipline, acting upon objects or people, helps them function once more according to the original intent.

The equipping sense of the word is shown in Hebrews 13:21, an exhortation that God "equip (discipline) you with everything good that you may do his will, working in you that which is pleasing in his sight." Through discipline we receive the means to accomplish our Lord's purpose. Equipping discipline comes from an external source; i.e., one is equipped from without with whatever is necessary to fulfill a given task.

Discipline corrects error. When things happen which are wrong, discipline is applied for correction. "My son, do not regard lightly the discipline (*paideuo*) of the Lord, nor lose courage when you are punished by him."[2] Note that discipline is not retributive. One is not punished in payment for doing wrong. Rather, it is applied positively for correction and prevention.

Training or education is another meaning inherent in the word. In order for the right things to happen, discipline as education is applied. " 'For the Lord disciplines him who he loves.' "[3] The *Jerusalem Bible* renders the verb discipline (*paideuo*) "train." "For the Lord trains the ones that he loves." The implication is that divine discipline molds us into being and doing that which God desires. Our job is to cooperate with the Lord's disciplining and not lose heart when it is applied. Disciplined training is necessary in all worthwhile endeavors, whether aviation, medicine, music, or the Christian life.

One submits to the rigors of a specific discipline to become skilled in that activity. Disciplined training requires dedication and determination to pursue one's goal, often at great personal sacrifice. Athletes in training for Olympic competition expend huge amounts of time, effort, and money in the pursuit of the gold medal. With a singlemindedness that borders on fanaticism, contenders put everything they have into a determined effort to achieve. Personal habits, diet, sleep, exercise, mental outlook, along with systematic coaching are carefully regulated and controlled. The path to great skill and excellence in world-class competition is discipline; without it, little is accomplished.

Discipline is a normal God-ordered method for bringing us into the maturity that God envisions for the redeemed. Discipleship means participating in, cooperating with, and acting upon insights that work to perfect Christian character. Discipline dynamically restores that which has gone amiss; it equips us for doing better, corrects error, and educates us in the achievement of biblical goals. It is the key to a maturing music ministry.

Reaffirming Monastic Life

The deadening effects of autonomous and undisciplined self-indulgence in the twentieth century has not gone unnoticed. In a limited way the Roman Catholic Church and some Protestants have responded to this peril by reaffirming the basic principles of medieval monasticism. Newly established communities, as well as the continuation of older monastic orders (all governed under some type of disciplined rule), have given Christians an alternative to the self-indulgent life. The emphasis was put on great gospel truths: simplicity of life, biblical conservatism, and submissive humility. More was found in less, richness was discovered in leanness. Discipline—both personal and corporate—held life together. Imposed on and accepted by each person, discipleship was the key to meaningful living.

Such disciplined living is not anti-pleasure as such. Rather, put in a biblical perspective, restraint enhances pleasure. For example, one would think that if one chocolate tasted good, a whole box would be that much better. Not so. In gorging we find that indulgence deadens the senses, a blandness sets in. Taste becomes tastelessness and pleasure turns into a stomach ache. Temperance is the way to true enjoyment, a fact not lost on the communities which have been formed to rediscover disciplined living. It is paradoxical: freedom is to be found within limits; in weakness we are strong; the last will be first.

Simplicity and spareness produce the best results in the long run. The account in Daniel 1 of the four young men's preparation for service in Nebuchadnezzar's palace is most instructive. Although the king gave instructions that their diet consist of the rich food and drink from his own table, Daniel prevailed upon the steward to serve only vegetables and water. Subsequent to a trial period of ten days, they "looked healthier and were better nourished than all the young men who had lived on the food assigned them by the king." After three years, Nebuchadnezzar found none to compare with the four and chose them to enter his employ.

We are indebted to many religious communities for bringing before the larger church elements of a more biblical model for living than that provided by general culture. The ascetic life espoused by religious communities and those who have taken holy orders is most compelling. In an age with no anchor except its own subjectivity, the time is right for reexamining the tenets of monastic/biblical Christian living. It is revealing that in 1988 three respected theologians—John Stott, Richard Halverson, and Richard Mouw—advocated the "remonking" of the church. Stott stated that "if he were young and beginning his Christian discipleship over, he would establish a kind of evangelical monastic order." Halverson would move toward the simplicity of the Hutterians, and Mouw would opt for a monastic-like order which would call the entire church to a more radical witness.[4]

The call to rethink our entire Christian culture is here. We need to take advantage of the example provided by the church's monastic brother and sisterhoods. They have something vital to teach us. In light of contemporary culture they seem absolutely out of step. They are. But that's the point. They seem radical because we have allowed secular concepts more than biblical ones to order our living. The church faces danger when its witness in the world becomes so inoffensive that any sharp contrast between it and the world fades. In an eloquent testimonial to the power of Christian asceticism, W. Paul Jones writes:

> These monks in this place are subversives, not so much because of what they say or even think, but what they are. In the midst of a culture of noise, these little white-robed men who like to play with bells choose silence; in a culture of work, they choose contemplation; in a culture of self-realization, they renounce the self; in a culture of achievement, they declare that the winner will be loser and only the loser winner; in a culture whose economy is utterly dependent on consumption, they insist on emptiness; in a culture structured by possession, they insist upon detachment; in a culture intoxicated by facts and education, they insist on ignorance as the basis of wisdom; in a culture of complexity they call us to the simplicity of willing one thing; in a culture intent on a high standard of living they insist on a high standard of life. Achievement versus grace; the exposure of the emptiness of fullness for the fullness of emptiness.[5]

Discipled living will, at the least, provide clear options to a world which is seeking itself and finding nothing there.

The discipline of living ascetically requires a whole new thought process, new orientation, and above all, a new approach to the practics of music and ministry in worship. A true discipleship will cause battle lines to be redrawn and priorities to be reordered. Church music ministry will work for the long-term good of its constituency rather than for their immediate gratification.

A Balanced Asceticism

A thoroughgoing discipleship has an equilibrium that avoids extremes, emphasizing necessity instead of indulgence, simplicity rather than extravagance, spareness instead of excess, clarity not garishness, creativity in place of banality, straightforwardness rather than sentimentality, and honesty above manipulation. The heart of Christian discipleship is biblical leanness. This is not to suggest grim harshness, denial of the goodness of creation, or self-righteousness which revels in pain. Rather, the essential goodness of life is affirmed with a certain conservative restraint. The Christian way to live life fully and wholeheartedly is to deny the flesh and be a pilgrim. Disciples travel light but not lightheaded, they live simply but not simplistically. Facing the future with courage and serenity, instead of bravado or naiveté, gives them the pilgrim's balance between complete renunciation of the world and a complete endorsement of it. While mature Christians must scrupulously avoid hedonism, they also know the gift of life in God's world is not some kind of terrestrial torture to be endured.. The beautiful thing is that when we practice integrity, honesty, truthfulness, simplicity, and straightforwardness in our living, we discover a satisfaction that goes beyond what the wider culture can offer. Disciples are neither flagellants nor revelers, but biblical ascetics.

Delayed Gratification

Discipleship rests on an assumption basic to many fields of study (e.g., psychology, religion, aesthetics, ethics, and morality): the concept of delayed gratification. Though secularism has largely rejected it in favor of immediate gratification, its importance remains. The principle here is that delaying gratification heightens value, while immediate gratification has the reverse

effect. In aesthetics the process of delaying artistic consumma-
tion, that is, delaying the gratification of arriving at a work's
cadential goals in the most immediate, direct, and straightforward manner, give to the work its objective artistic worth.
Very small children soon learn that saving the frosting till last
enhances appreciation. We find delayed gratification in nature.
Apple trees don't bear fruit until the tree is in its maturity, and
then only months after the blossoms are set. Waiting is part of
God's economy.

In the twentieth century, the importance of this principle
was lessened as extreme humanistic philosophy infiltrated society. A whole culture sprang up with a passion for instantaneous
satisfaction. Norms centuries old were circumvented in an attempt to attain one's ends in the most immediate and direct
fashion. Painting by numbers produced instant "works of art,"
piano instruction in ten easy lessons produced "skilled pianists"!
Chord organs produced "harmony" and "rhythm" from the
touch of a button. Moral law was reduced to doing what felt
good. "Ethics" became a fancy word for expediency. This climate
made normal the pursuit of "doing one's own thing," without
responsibility and without regard for the consequences. Discipline was abandoned.

Contrast with the World

The contrast of biblical discipline with worldly license is
stark. Whereas culture has opted for lawlessness, God still asks
his disciples to pay the price of following him. No greater symbol
of this can be found than that of the cross. It reminds us that a
disciple must expect crucifixion, and only in losing one's life will
life be truly found.[6] In Luke 9:57–62 Jesus tells his disciples that
following him takes priority above everything else: "Leave the
dead to bury their own dead. No one who puts his hand to the
plough and looks back is fit for the kingdom of God." The
Epistles continue in the same vein. Peter is typical, enumerating
standards of conduct which, though they are high, can reason-
ably be expected of Christian disciples.[7] The cost and requirements of discipleship cannot be easily dismissed. God calls us to
a radical obedience that demands sacrifice. Only as we follow him
in all our behavior will our witness be effective in the undisciplined world in which we live.

The Christians of the Early Church

Early Christians knew that the plight of Stephen, the first martyr, might be their experience as well. Temporal life was uncertain with "Maranatha, Lord, Come!" the great rallying cry. These new believers were put to the test many times. Beaten, tortured, and killed, they maintained their distinctive Christian witness and faithfully approached living in terms of soldiering. Hardship, struggle, and suffering for the cause of Christ marked their discipleship.

The *Teaching of the Twelve Apostles* (the *Didache*, written between the years AD 80 and 200) was a document of instruction, a condensed rule for life and living to guide new converts.[8] It was specific about maintaining the highest Christian standards, containing no "if you feel that," or "as you wish," or "if you like." The *Didache* clearly states that the Christian life must be a disciplined life. Origen (AD 183–252) in *Against Celsus* also notes that initiation into the Christian community was well regulated: "Individuals are taught as hearers, and only when they have given ample proof that they want to lead a good life are they introduced into the community. Some of the Christians are appointed to watch over the lives and appraise the conduct of those who want to join them."[9] Hippolytus (ca. AD 175–236), writing in *The Apostolic Tradition*, gives clear indication that the living of new Christians is carefully scrutinized. Certain occupations, habits, and behavioral patterns are not worthy of the Lord and therefore not tolerated.[10] Fledgling bands of believers established helps for disciplined behavior in the manner of "rules" for living. It took discipline to resist the wiles of pagan culture since it was neither easy nor popular to become a "follower of the Way." Christians

> live in their own countries, but only as guests and aliens. They take part in everything as citizens and endure everything as aliens. Every foreign country is their homeland, and every homeland is a foreign country to them. They marry like everyone else. They beget children, but they do not expose them after they are born. They have a common table, but no common bed. They are in the flesh, but they do not live according to the flesh. They live on earth, but their citizenship is in Heaven. They obey the established laws, but through their way of life they surpass these laws.[11]

Discipline and Maturity

Discipline Produces Maturity

Leanness, austerity, and discipline produce maturity. "Shallow, soft religion with comfort and prosperity as its objectives is not only inadequate . . . it is treasonable."[12] We should never try to make the expressions of our faith so sugary sweet and comfortable that pleasure is the primary result. Such indulgent expressions do not produce Christians who have the health and stamina to be disciples. While perhaps in ways more subtle than in antiquity, our world is every bit as pagan, cruel, and inhospitable to the gospel as that of the first three centuries. Religion that is "nice," "acceptable," and "comfy," is impotent and without significant meaning. We need to practice a theism which is comprehensively disciplined, cutting across the lines of theology, sociology, ethics, aesthetics, and morality. If we do not, our word symbols will say one thing, but our deeds, actions, and forms (including music) will say quite another.

Motivation for Discipline

Motivation for discipline is effective over the long haul as we exercise true agape love toward God, loving him selflessly. Agape love goes far beyond any legalistic obligation we may feel toward Christ's call. Loving God is such a powerful force that nothing in heaven or earth can overcome it. We serve him because we love him.

Discipline is a narrow gate and a hard way. It is God's way to a rich and full life, earthly yet heavenly, temporal yet eternal. In his wisdom he knows what is good for us. The key to discipline is to rid self of its innate willfulness. If we could accept the premise that God knows more about us than we do and requires discipline because he loves us, then our whole perspective would change. Christian discipline would then cease to be an albatross and become a feather.

Discipline, Music, and Worship

Christian discipleship depends on a balanced ascetic restraint, motivated by agape love. Nowhere is such discipline needed more than in the music of worship. If we are to provide an alternative to hedonism and develop mature Christians, worship music must become more disciplined. Attempting to follow the disciplined life of a disciple, yet wallowing in self-indulgent worship, weakens the believer immensely. The forms used in worship help determine the level of a believer's maturity by being disciplined forms themselves. A comprehensive and thoroughgoing discipleship must principle our music since the music we use stamps its own image on us.

Notes

1. John 13:15–16 (RSV).
2. Hebrews 12:5 (RSV).
3. Hebrews 12:6 (RSV).
4. Rodney Clapp, "Remonking the Church," *Christianity Today*, 12 August 1988, 20.
5. W. Paul Jones, *The Province Beyond the River* (New York: Paulist, 1981), vii.
6. Mark 8:34–38 (RSV).
7. 1 Peter 1:13–25 (RSV).
8. Eberhard Arnold, *The Early Christians* (Grand Rapids: Baker, 1979), 14, 323.
9. Origen, *Against Celsus* 3.51, quoted in Arnold, *The Early Christians*, 323.
10. Ibid., 108.
11. *Letter to Diognetus* 5,6 quoted in Arnold, *The Early Christians*, 109.
12. Samuel Shoemaker, "The Way of the Cross," *Cross Point* 2 (Spring 1989): 17.

Discipling Music Ministry

The phrase "discipling music ministry" will be investigated in this chapter in two interrelated ways. We will look into those characteristics which discipline church music and those which give music (and music ministry) its potential for being a discipling agent. We will also examine the characteristics of a discipling music program, one which has as its goal the maturing of the believer.

Characteristics of Disciplined Music

Church music, like any other activity, is able to take on characteristics which go beyond the meaning of the thing itself. Music can be sad, happy, creative, weak, banal, fulfilling, rebellious, or any number of other characteristics. It may be martial, solemn, or dancelike, and it can engender in the listener patriotism, nostalgia, or school spirit. Whenever a composer creates a composition, a statement is made. The idiosyncratic features of each composition give to it a distinct personality, a singularity. Regardless of text, the general feeling tone of notes, rhythms, and harmonies builds a musical ethos which becomes an agent in our maturing or immaturing.

Musical Grammar Affects Maturity

Music which is built upon immature theoretical concepts fosters a similar condition in the listener. For example, banality and triteness are musical characteristics associated with the lightness and airiness of the more popular types of music. To the extent church music (which represents gospel meaning) is principled by such attributes, it influences the worshiper to a like banality and triteness—not just musically, but spiritually as well. A whole life (holistic) spiritual maturity is affected by the church music we ingest. Just as what we read affects our entire life, so the music we listen to influences us. Not that this is automatic, for there are many variables at work here. But it must be acknowledged that a mature church music is a powerful force in the maturation of Christians.

Musical Vocabulary

The music director must know what makes music disciplined so that competent choices can be made. It is useless to believe that one ought to use disciplined music and at the same time be unaware of the criteria on which such selection rests. Merely agreeing that discipline is necessary to the maturing process is not enough! Good intentions must be actualized by an informed musical vocabulary. The music director must have the ability and skill to analyze the meaning inherent in vocabulary and syntax. Ministerial intent is thwarted unless the music actually says what the director intends.

Music, like all languages, is a cultural phenomenon. Its meanings are determined within the structure of the society in which it exists. For us, Western civilization is the larger parameter within which referential meaning operates. Oriental or African scales, rhythms, melodies, harmonies, and instruments are foreign to us. Their sounds are so outside our experience that we are largely unable to make anything of them at all. For a Westerner to understand and appreciate Eastern music, one would literally have to be immersed in the culture long enough to assimilate it.

For those within the domain of Western civilization, meanings are understood within its inferential framework. Though there are universal musical principles common to all cultures, our specific understanding is limited by the unique set of musical reference points which govern our culture's music. Though we may not like or agree with them, they are operative anyway, since they are assumptions which we cannot change. Actually, this is not surprising, for a cultural language which had no basic grammar would be so incomprehensible that it would never rise to any importance at all. It would amount to gibberish. So, with a fair degree of accuracy, we are able to draw some acceptable general statements about music within our own cultural milieu. Certain descriptive words can be used definitively to fit stipulated musical circumstances. For example, we say fast music has energy, slow music is more languid. The interval of a third is more consonant than that of a seventh. Consonances are agreeable, dissonances somewhat chafing. Music which has a heavy beat is driving, while the opposite is flowing. Likewise, when we talk about musical discipline it will be within the given understandings of Western culture.

Harmony

In general, music is disciplined to the extent that it moves toward the ascetic. Harmony which is lean, spare, and rather austere is a more disciplined harmony than the lavish and rich harmonies of the super-romanticists, the sweetish supper club harmonies of added and parallel seconds, sixths, ninths, and thirteenths, or those associated with barbershop quartet music with their parallel rising dominant sevenths. These do not have the bite we expect in a disciplined music. Rigor, pungency, and straightforwardness are better suited to ministry than lassitude, sweetness, and insipidness.

Open fourths and fifths work as an astringent. This is demonstrated by the following harmonization of "What Wondrous Love Is This." Observe the rigorous harmony of example 1.

Note the preponderance of open fourths and fifths. Its rather austere character makes it a disciplined setting. The same tune harmonized without open fourths, fifths, and octaves, however, gives a much less stark impression. The harmony of example 2 is "nicer" and more "likeable." But it is also the less disciplined of the two settings.

Another case in point is the harmonization of "Now, My Tongue, the Mystery Telling." Example 3 utilizes tertian harmony, while example 4 is a good bit more chaste and ascetic, with harmony that is most noticeably more open in its embracing of chords without the third.

It should also be said that the most disciplined rendition of this hymn is one without any harmony at all, i.e., unaccompanied. Then the plainsong tune will be at its best.

Compare the familiar "How Firm a Foundation" sung to the tune *Foundation*, examples 5 and 6. Notice that example 5 is fully decked out in four part harmony, complete with dominant sevenths in two of its four cadences. Example 6, on the other hand, is a good bit more "rough and ready," more severe, and more resolute. Its unvarnished pungency gives the words superb support. It is the more disciplined setting.

Rhythm

Rhythm, the basis of music (music being a time art), must also be disciplined. It is interesting to note that the seventeenth- and early eighteenth-century practice of ironing out the rugged rhythms of the sixteenth-century German chorales is currently being reevaluated. There is an awareness that the hale and hardy drive of the original is a much more authentic musical statement for carrying the Reformation disposition than the watered-down, "improved," even-quarter-note versions of a century later. The original is more difficult to sing, especially at first, but the effort is well worth it. The original rhythm empowers the text of the hymn in a most remarkable fashion. The Reformation spirit was one of energy and exhilaration. "A Mighty Fortress Is Our God" is a chorale of action, not sedation. Textually, this clearly appears in the translation used in the 1978 *Lutheran Book of Worship*.[1] God is a fortress, but also our sword and shield—implements of offense. We are engaged in a battle. Satan is our foe and Jesus Christ our champion. Armed with "weapons of the Spirit" we are overcomers through Christ our Lord. Musically, the excitement and force of the text comes through best in the original rough-hewn rhythm. Compare example 7 with example 8, noting the staid rhythmic regularity of the former and the dynamic energy of the latter.

In church music, rhythm is not as disciplined as it ought to be when it imparts a sense of jolly toe-tapping swing. While not denying the importance of bodily involvement in worship, it is fair to say that rhythm which is so compelling that bodily movement is invariably the result, takes attention away from the text (and from the subject of the text—God). When hymns are so rhythmically irresistible that hand-clapping, dancing, or patty-caking is the routine response, we may be having fun, but such songs are ultimately self-defeating. Any music that has an over-bearing rhythmic drive which induces excess and unrestrained bodily response pleasures the self. It gives "me" a rollicking good time. But it lacks the discipline necessary for maturation. When attention is riveted to fleshly response, then church music has succumbed to an infantile self-centeredness.

The following two hymns illustrate different settings of the same text, the first (example 9) evidencing a frolicsome, rhythmic looseness, and the second (example 10) a controlled, yet cheerful, rhythmic discipline.

Generally whenever rhythm engenders a response that attracts us to attend to our own feelings and desires, it detracts from worship and works against the maturing of God's saints. The hedonistic spirit becomes the dominant spirit. The worshiper is turned inward, invariably leading to the entertainment of the self.

Melody

The way melody is crafted also adds to the overall impression of discipline or the lack of it. The use of non-diatonic (chromatic) tones which are decorative give tunes a certain syrupy quality. When used extensively, these melodies lose the sinewy quality that discipline requires. Such chromaticism attempts to be expressive without travail. It is surface ornamentation, incidental to the internal workings of the music. Its light and frothy effervescence lacks seriousness of purpose. Although perfect for many other roles, it fails in worship. Notice the chromaticism in example 11.

Another example is "O Little Town of Bethlehem." When set to the familiar tune "St. Louis" (example 12), it is not as strong as when set to "Forest Green" (example 13). The chromaticism in "St. Louis," as well as the many parallel sixths, gives the tune a rather sweet and cloying feeling absent in "Forest Green." The latter is the more disciplined of the two.

Another melodic trait which shows a lack of discipline is extreme internal repetition, giving the music a dull and stereotyped character. It is as if the composer determined to hypnotically capture one's attention on the first hearing (immediate gratification) so that subsequent repetitions would be reflexive and automatic. Such music, though boring, is highly accessible. Unfortunately, it is too accessible, exuding a juvenile or immature character which shapes the worshiper exactly in that same frame of reference. Look at example 14.

Notice that the stanzas and the refrains both utilize two repeated phrases. Both change the endings of their respective second phrase. This amount and type of repetition is not the problem. The most devastating blow to the song's creative discipline is the internal repetition of the dotted eighth and sixteenth notes as found in measure one, and in the opening motif of the refrain. The rhythmic and melodic figures are reiterated over and over without relief of development. Compare measure two and three with measure one, and notice the derivative sameness of measures two and three and subsequent measures. Such melodic construction gives new meaning to the word "cliché"! The musical discipline necessary for use in a maturing ministry is absent. This melody is sure to have other uses, but it lacks the toughness of a maturing tool.

Another case of extreme repetition is found in example 15. The entire song is built around the motifs in measures one and two. Notice that each measure is a conspicuous repetition or sequence of measure one or measure two. The cadences of each phrase are melodically similar and are derivations of the motif in bar one. It is a monotonous tune, highly predictable and tedious.

Such melodic structure is not uncommon in many of the choruses, songs, gospel arrangements, and anthems that we use. It is something music directors need to watch out for. Though not necessarily as extreme as the above examples, there is more dull melody in church music than we care to admit. The best composition has enough melodic variety to keep it from being shallow, yet enough repetition to keep it from fragmentation. Melody based on monotony is poor music, unusable in a maturing ministry of music.

Polyphony

One of the most disciplined types of melody writing is polyphony. It features a texture in which the soprano, alto, tenor, or bass parts are quite independent melodically, yet combine to form a consonant harmony. Polyphony (or counterpoint—point against point, note against note) requires skilled writing. The challenge is to keep the melodic interest primary, while insuring that the resulting harmony retains a viability in its own right.

The church can advantageously utilize such music. Polyphony has a certain rigor and strength which results from its compositional distinctives. The words of such music are difficult to grasp because they are not sung simultaneously in each part. It is not meant, however, to be a type of message music such as that found in a solo song. Rather, the music itself is largely the message as it musically explores the inner meaning of the text.

Polyphonic texture has a spirit about it which is kin to the transcendental nature of God. It is not as "immanent" or immediately apprehensible as homophony (one main tune with supporting harmony, such as that found in a hymn). The compositional remoteness and disciplined distance of polyphony give to the music a certain ambiguity which reminds us of God's distance, his dissimilarity to us. Though made in his image, people are really not "chips off the old block." God is different from us, far above us, removed and remote from us. We cannot approach him. It is he who must come to us. A clear understanding of God's transcendence expressed in the musical texture of polyphony helps us avoid a too familiar and radical immanence in which God becomes a personal genie to do our bidding. Counterpoint redresses the exaggeration of the overfamiliar God of the name-it, claim-it religionists. Polyphony's disposition is decidedly otherworldly.

Insights from the Church's Heritage

Rhythmic Development

Historically, rhythm was always very carefully treated by the church. Music of the early church and the medieval period was largely unmeasured; that is, it did not rigidly distinguish between lengths of notes. But gradually, from about the eleventh to the end of the sixteenth century, rhythm became measured (mensural rhythm), although it had no metrical accents or bar lines to divide music into groupings with unvarying rhythmic pulses. When church music eventually opted for a more precise rhythm, rhythmic modes and mensural notation of various kinds were developed: primitive notation (c. 900–1150), square notation (c. 1175–1225), pre-Franconian notation (c. 1225–1275), black mensural notation (c. 1250–1450), and white mensural notation (c. 1450–1600). Not until the beginning of the Baroque period (about 1600) did metrical rhythm become an accepted practice.

Humanism and Rhythm

Renaissance humanism gave impetus to the gradual shift from a non-metrical rhythm to a metrical one. A free-flowing unmetrical rhythm did not have the catchy, bouncy, earth-stomping quality essential for emphasis on self-pleasure, one of the Renaissance's fledgling concerns. Of course, the dance always utilized the metrical idea of simultaneous, regularly recurring stresses throughout the musical texture. Church music did not. However it was the dance which served as the basis for much musical development during and subsequent to the Renaissance. At present, metrical rhythm is so ingrained in our musical consciousness that the average person can hardly imagine music without it. We need to be aware, however, that it was the humanistic tendency to delight the self that led to church music's embracing of meter in the first place. That should tell us something—an emphasis on human pleasure is served by a strong repetitive rhythm.

Melodic and Harmonic Genesis—The Church Modes

Scales form the basis of all melody and harmony. Although there are many different scales, at present only two are generally used in Western music—Major and Minor. It was not always so. Until 1600 the medieval church modes were the established sources of scalar material. Today this modal system offers much to the contemporary musician who is searching for a disciplined music valuable in ministry.

A mode is a scale. Each mode has a different whole and half step combination. A distillation of the church music of the Middle Ages shows that the scale basis of the chant and the centonization (the process of connecting often-used melodic fragments) of its melodies, utilized eight different step and half-step combinations. In his *Dodecachordon* of 1547, Glarean, a sixteenth-century theorist, added to these eight church modes the Ionian (Major) and Aeolian (Minor) scales.

The step and half-step arrangement of two of the church modes can be seen in the following examples. The Dorian mode in example 16 and the Phrygian mode in example 17 each have a different sequence of steps and half steps. It is these varying stepwise arrangements which give each mode its distinctive flavor. Playing these scales on the piano will demonstrate the musical character of each.

Pieces based on a church mode will tend to have those characteristics which listeners term austere, stringent, or pungent, qualities which in their antiseptic way will help scrub sensuous pleasure from being the listener's most immediate reaction to the music. Modal composition has a somewhat similar quality to that based on the natural minor scale. Of course the exact aesthetic difference is considerable. But for those who have only major and minor to use as a frame of reference, modal music comes closer to minor, though the church modes are still more stark. The modes are one help in removing the centrality of musical pleasure as the basis for choice, helping sensitize believers to more important concerns in worship.

The following are illustrative of modal discipline. The first tune (example 18) is in the hypomixolydian mode, the second (example 19) in the dorian. It is interesting to compare the modal setting of "All Glory, Laud, and Honor," example 19, with the major setting, example 20. Notice how much more ascetic the modal version is than the major version.

Humanistic Influences on Melody and Harmony

In the context of our study, it is significant to realize that the Major scale, the one now preferred, came into prominence during the Renaissance shift from a more God-centered perspective to a more ego-centered one. The worldview of the Renaissance drastically affected the modal system of the Middle Ages. That the Major scale became the favorite of composers and listeners alike is attested to by its domination of Western music for the last four hundred years. The issue is not that the scale basis of music changed, but the attending reasons why the modal system was gradually abandoned in favor of the major-minor system.

It was the inward concentration on the pleasing of self which increasingly caused composers to focus on the Major scale. As the unity of life built upon God and the church broke up, and self and self-pleasure became preeminent, the Major scale gained ascendancy. The reason was simple. The Major scale was more satisfying to the individual than the medieval modes. Tickling the listener's fancy more, it gave a greater measure of delight. The times gradually legitimized the view that people and their feelings took priority over the church and its discipline. Deryck Cooke in *The Language of Music* notes that Major

> belonged to the popular, secular life founded on the desire for pleasure; and this always threatened to undermine the religious ideal of a humble, God-centered existence, in which the emphasis was on the acceptance of one's lot in "this vale of tears," and to replace it by the concept of a proud, man-centered existence, in which the emphasis was on personal happiness.[2]

Over the years the church had been aware of the secularizing trends in church music prompted by the desire to pleasure self. As early as the fourteenth century there was concern that the church modes were beginning to lose their hold. Nevertheless, the church resisted the drift to a single major-minor system for three hundred more years. But by 1600 the battle was lost, and the church modes were largely dropped. The church, of course, perpetuated them to the extent it used Gregorian chant and the medieval psalm tones. But other than an occasional flashback, composers largely ignored them.

The development of tertian harmony (harmony based on the interval of a third) also parallels the development of humanism. This was quite significant. Harmony, until about 1400, was based on the intervals of the octave, fifth, and fourth (quartal harmony). Thirds were considered dissonant. The system was derived from the natural harmonic series in which the second, third, and fourth harmonics produce the interval of an octave, fifth, and fourth when sounded with each harmonic's respective predecessor. Because of their primary position in nature's overtone series these intervals were given prominence in the harmonic structure of the music. But during the Renaissance the third became more important, until by 1600 tertian harmony dominated the harmonic system.

Part of the reason thirds became favored is that Renaissance people were fonder of them than the more severe octaves, fifths, or fourths. Although thirds and sixths (an inversion of thirds) had been normal in medieval secular music, the medieval church eschewed them because of its reluctance to allow pleasure to become a determinative factor in worship and life. But during the Renaissance an increasingly secular society eroded the church's position. Human pleasure became a prime motive for change.

The suggestion that a resurgence of modal usage and medieval quartal harmony in the church would be one way to introduce a more disciplined, dispassionate, and objective approach to church music is historically compelling. Even as a move toward the more pleasurable Major scale and tertian harmony heralded a like societal move, so a move away from them might give birth to a less pleasure-driven compulsion, especially in worship. The problem, of course, is not simply the problem of pleasure, but pleasure as an end in itself. Though good in its place and in proper perspective, pleasure gets out of hand when it is primary. Church music which is eliminated because it is not pleasurable enough merely demonstrates how caught up we are in the hedonism of society. Pleasure ought not be the sole criteria for that which is valuable or useful. Frankly, it is the affinity for sobriety, purity, and refinement which makes modality and medieval open harmony useful to us in our present age. The church modes are uncharacteristic of our time in much the same way that a thoroughgoing biblical Christianity is uncharacteristic of our society. That modal scales and harmony are not popular is not a reason to shun them. Indeed, this may indicate our need for them.

Monotonic Recitation

There is one type of musical setting so spare that a majority of churches have largely abandoned it—monotonic recitation. It is simple and unadorned, the declamation of text in a prose rhythm mostly sung to a single note. Cantillation, as it is sometimes called, is extremely useful in church because large quantities of text, such as entire psalms, canticles, or other biblical passages, can be sung without paraphrasing the text to fit a particular musical meter.

Monotonic recitation and its accompanying forms (such as the Gregorian and Sarum psalm tones) avoid the awkward problems of fitting prose texts to meter and rhythm. The entire passage may be sung to one single note, or, in the case of the psalm tones, one note with an opening intonation (inititum) and a concluding termination (cadence). A short example of mono-tonic recitation from Psalm 141:2a is shown in example 21.

The simplicity of cantillation insures that one's attention can be riveted entirely on the meaning of the text. This combi-nation of text and music gives both listener and singer time to reflect on the words. We are not so caught up with musical beauty that the text becomes superfluous. Sung text tends to be more deliberate and paced than just saying the text. The old adage, "He who sings prays twice," is most certainly true here. It is well to remember that for most of Christian history almost everything in worship, including prayers and scripture readings, were sung, seldom spoken! Much of it utilized some type of cantillation.

Monotonic recitation is a type of exercise which calls for a certain measure of discipline on the part of all participants. This is not a music for music's sake. It is a purely functional music. Its economy and utter simplicity give it an unostentatious quality very much in keeping with the spirit of the gospel. Not widely acclaimed, it has no "tune," no "rhythm," no "beat." The very things which our culture so admires in music are absent. Indeed that is why it can be so useful in a discipling music ministry. Such music may help counteract the hedonistic tendencies of our culture by recalling us to that which is not entertaining, but nourishing; not self-indulgent, but beneficial; not intemperate, but wholesome. The cross of Christ can be clearly seen in the music's simplicity, plainness, and lack of sophistication. It can discipline church music into returning to essentials, emphasizing purity, modesty, and true humility.

Gregorian Chant

More elaborate than cantillation, Gregorian chant is a veritable gold mine of disciplined church music. It was named in honor of St. Gregory (c. 540–604), who was influential in collecting and codifying the church's song of the early centuries into a useable and manageable body of material. There are many types of chant (also termed plainsong or plainchant) depending upon style, liturgical usage, and method of performance. Though much of plainchant's ancestry has been clouded by passing centuries, and though we cannot know its history with flawless accuracy, available evidence suggests that much of the church's plainchant came from Hebrew sources.[3] Gregorian chant is closer than we realize to the music sung by the twelve disciples, the apostles, and our Lord himself. We would expect it to have the disciplined character necessary for carrying out the biblical mandate of making disciples.

Plainchant is a type of music which specifically belongs to the church. It has lasted now for some two thousand years. Though sharply curtailed because of the Second Vatican Council's emphasis on relevancy, it is still a viable musical form for our time. In fact, it is one of the best disciplined musical forms available for ministry today. Though plainchant was originally composed for the Latin language, there is little reason why the vernacular (English, for example) cannot be used.

The tremendous vitality and timelessness of plainchant comes from the fact that it is not bound to the changing whims and fashions of the temporal. With an otherworldly orientation, chant's locus of being is in the spiritual. Not made for beauty, aesthetic contemplation, enjoyment, pleasure, or emotional satisfaction, it is uniquely different from the way we have come to think of music.

Plainchant is foreign to our post-Christian culture. Such music, though out of step with the values of our age, can help reorder them in such a way that they are governed by the eternal, not the temporal, and center around God rather than self. Lamenting the loss of Gregorian chant, Joseph Sittler notes:

> The old stance of the church that floats with a timeless, high impersonality—this is the very essence of the Christian God-relationship. This was before I was; this will be when I am gone. God's initiative toward me does not hang on the vagaries of my subjectivity. There is something in the old chants of the church that brought a necessary, audible balance to the self-incurvature of contemporary Christianity.[4]

The Music of Plainchant

With its limited and circumspect movement, plainchant is not melodically extravagant. Its thriftiness in the utilization of musical raw material shows good stewardship of what we might feel are quite limited resources. Yet its poverty is its richness; its melodic spareness is a reminder that God can multiply even a few musical loaves and fishes. The discipleship of limitations yields bountiful results.

The precise rhythmic (and melodic) performance practices of medieval chant may be an insoluble problem due to lack of hard evidence. Nevertheless, the Benedictine monks of the Abbey of Solesmes, France, did much in the nineteenth and twentieth centuries to interpret and transcribe the chant in a manner consistent with the reverent spirit of medieval worship. The Solesmes usage, based upon their *Paleographie musicale*, is the generally accepted way of singing Gregorian chant. In making their work available to musicians in their many publications, they have done much to make its performance uniform. Their writings not only include the chants themselves, but contain instructive helps in interpreting notation. Their transcriptions favor all notes being of equal value with only a few exceptions. Other scholars believe that because the square notation of Gregorian chant was not particularly precise, a more rhythmic interpretation is possible.

Though we are not exactly sure of all of the intricacies of the rhythm of chant, we can depend on the best scholarship to point out that a strong steady driving beat was never one of its characteristics. The rhythm was much more the accentuation of the text with an absence of regularly recurring metrical pulsations. The result of having no metrical beats is a music which floats more than it is propelled, soars rather than being thrust. The lack of rhythmic kick gives a disciplined reserve in keeping with the timelessness of the eternal. Rigid temporality is absent because of the variable flow of rhythmic groupings. The smooth and easy movement, having no metrical propulsion, gives us a fleeting glimpse into another world. This free-flowing rhythm is more akin to the timeless pace of heaven than to the rigid timeliness of earth.

The power of plainchant comes from its absolute incorruptibility, purity, and guilelessness. The absence of manipulative purpose provides an innocence suitable for the holy. Contemporary listeners may initially think of chant as dull and boring, lacking the excitement he or she is used to. It has no beat, no harmony, little color, and no accompaniment. Even the melody is quite out of keeping with present compositional practice. Given time, understanding, and familiarity, however, listeners discover plainchant to be almost sublime. When we begin over again, stripping away our musical and religious prejudices, this music has a freshness which is astounding. Calm and serene, disciplined yet free, chant makes a convincing musical medium for promoting a reverential God-centered worship. The very lack of fleshly appeal makes it a good musical tool for encouraging holistic maturity in the believer.

Restraint in Church Music

In general composers have always employed a more reserved style for music which depicts the spiritual (heaven, goodness, and virtue) than that used to depict the worldly (hell, evil, and depravity). In the formative years of the church, Christians were reminded to refrain from the fleshly music of pagan orgiastic rites and feasts, a music of excess and intemperance. Church edicts and pronouncements always took the conservative side of things. Churchmen were aware that music which was "too pleasing," was spiritually unhealthy. They strove mightily to keep the encroachments of secular musical culture from invading the church. The church's music was one of constraint. Even in the early Baroque, the division of musical styles shows church music to be the more moderate. *Stylus ecclesiasticus* or *prima prattica* referred to the more conservative style of composition. *Stylus cubicularias* included the less radical compositional elements of the *seconda prattica*; elements suited for madrigals, solo monody, and concerted works. The *stylus theatralis*, the most radical of all, encompasses the more daring of the *seconda prattica* innovations, a style especially appropriate to stage productions.

Until recently the church has generally agreed that boundaries, restraint, and decorum in its music was necessary. Practitioners opted for decency and order. Secular culture, however, tends toward shedding restraint and affirming license. Not that the church opted for the stodgy, the pallid, and the uninteresting, but it did, for the most part, seek to order its creativity in a tradition which emphasized gospel discipline and sobriety.

Today, the best composers continue to use musical practices which are more austere and remote when analogically representing virtue than when they are representing depravity. For example, Olivier Messiaen, though employing compositional devices in his devotional music far removed from tradition, exaggerates still further certain "violations of custom and of symmetry" when portraying evil and sin.[5] There seems to be built into the nature of things a calmness and order which we associate with the divine, and an opposite violence and unruliness characteristic of the flesh. This principle of restraint must not be lost on contemporary church music.

A Discipling Music Ministry

We have said that a discipling music ministry, one which takes seriously its duty to help the saints of God toward holistic spiritual maturity, uses as its basic maturing agent music which is disciplined. We have examined in the first section of this chapter some traits which make harmony, rhythm, and melody disciplined, and we have given a few examples of disciplined music. Unless the music of our calling is musically like the maturity we hope to advance in our people, the good intentions of the music director will be largely wasted. Congregations, pastors, and musicians must view music as the powerful agent the early church fathers and the reformers knew it to be. Let us not conclude that music is theoretically neutral as far as a worldview is concerned. Instead of allowing other priorities such as niceness, exuberance, likability, hilarity, religious feelings, or pleasure to be the determining factor in our choice of music, we must come to the place of accepting what advertisers, psychologists, composers of musical scores for movies, and pop rock musicians know: music is powerful, it influences, compels, educates, and disciples us. The church of Jesus Christ needs to look beyond the horizon; we must transcend the apparent. Discipline is just as much a key to music ministry as it is to life in general.

The insights gleaned from a look at humanism's influence on church music are disquieting. Though incalculable good has come from human creativity and ingenuity, we have seen that the compelling justification for much new development in music is the pleasuring of the self. That attitude taken to extreme in the twentieth century has given us a worship which often points inward. By learning what kinds of musical traits were characteristic of cultures whose focal point was God (such as medieval culture and the believers of the early church), we gain insight into the musical principles needed to achieve a similar end. A discipling music ministry must help the wider church to get back on track, to achieve a biblical balance in the music used in worship.

Such a ministry is concerned with lived-out faith. Imputing a cerebral theology apart from real life is not a goal of music ministry. In contrast, music ministry is a method of helping the assembly achieve a faith applicable to actual day-to-day living. It is a helping ministry, counteracting the debilitating effects of the major philosophical trends of our time through the discipline inherent in the music and by the judicious way that music is used.

In performing its rightful duties, music will often be a cause for complaint. Such is the consequence of any prophetic ministry. But adverse reactions do not mean particular ministry actions are necessarily wrong. If musicians act wisely, a certain amount of congregational pain is inevitable. Growth is often not pleasant. Moreover, we ought not feel guilty or have a sense of failure when we do not please everyone, since displeasure may be the exact catalyst God needs to help an individual mend such a disposition and become more spiritually mature. The undesirable reviews music directors receive may simply be the debris from the discipling actions of their ministry.

Take plainchant as an example. The fact that it is unpopular or irrelevant should not deter us from considering it. If we are convinced that such music, because of its many disciplined characteristics, should be used at some point, its unpopularity can be thought of positively. If chant is so unlikable that it causes people to become irrationally angry, such an attitude can be turned into good. Showing believers their need of a more Christ-like spirit is one small way music ministry may help people mature into the image of the Son. Stuffing ourselves with pleasurable musical experiences should not be characteristic of church worship. Moreover, chant will promote a more objective, faith-oriented Christian walk. The less dependent we are on subjective feeling, the more we learn to trust God as revealed in scripture. Chant's impersonal objectivity helps us achieve such growth.

Summary

All of God's people are called to be disciples. Further, it is discipline which makes a disciple. The potential of a music program for discipling the assembly is commensurate with its use of disciplined music and its implementation of a discipling music program. Church music becomes disciplined as it embraces artistic elements of delayed gratification, honesty, and integrity. It becomes undisciplined when it utilizes elements that make for easy acceptability and triteness.

Disciplined content in a church music program is crucial. Spiritual health is just as dependent upon discipline as is bodily health. Good physical fitness requires a constant battle between immediate and delayed gratification: french fries versus baked potatoes, sweets versus vegetables, inactivity versus exercise. We are what we ingest. Therefore, we should not expect that worship components can be designed so as to give worshipers that self-seeking pleasure satisfaction they so desperately crave and which culture leads them to believe is theirs by birthright, and yet produce Christians who are healthy. Maturity demands a depth in worship which musical forms based on the self-affirming secular humanism of our day are unable to fulfill. We must get out of the routine of fashioning our worship after assumptions which destroy the very faith we want to perpetuate. Only a thoroughgoing theism, in contradistinction to the other "isms" of society, complete with the discipline necessary for Christian discipleship, can make the church all that God intends it to be. The song of the faithful must be a disciplined song. As music incarnates Christian discipline, it disciples us after the very heart of God.

Example 1
What Wondrous Love Is This
From *The Hymnal 1982,* © Church Pension Fund. Used by permission.

Words: American folk hymn, ca. 1835
Music: *Wondrous Love,* from *The Southern Harmony,* 1835

12 9. 12. 12 9

Example 2
What Wondrous Love Is This

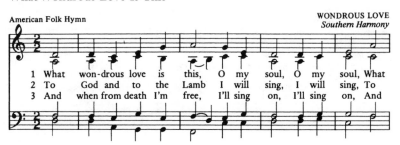

1 won-drous love is this, O my soul! What won-drous love is
2 God and to the Lamb I will sing; To God and to the
3 when from death I'm free, I'll sing on; And when from death I'm

1 this that caused the Lord of bliss To bear the dread-ful curse for my
2 Lamb, who is the great "I Am," While mil - lions join the theme, I will
3 free, I'll sing and joy - ful be, And through e - ter - ni - ty I'll sing

1 soul, for my soul, To bear the dread-ful curse for my soul!
2 sing, I will sing, While mil - lions join the theme, I will sing!
3 on, I'll sing on, And through e - ter - ni - ty I'll sing on!

Example 3
Now, My Tongue, the Mystery Telling
From *The Hymnal 1940*, © Church Pension Fund. Used by permission.

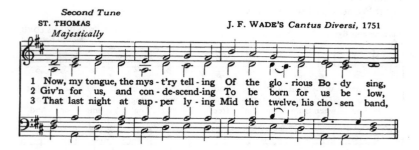

Second Tune
ST. THOMAS   J. F. WADE'S *Cantus Diversi*, 1751
Majestically

1 Now, my tongue, the mys - t'ry tell - ing Of the glo - rious Bo - dy sing,
2 Giv'n for us, and con - de-scend-ing To be born for us be - low,
3 That last night at sup - per ly - ing Mid the twelve, his cho - sen band,

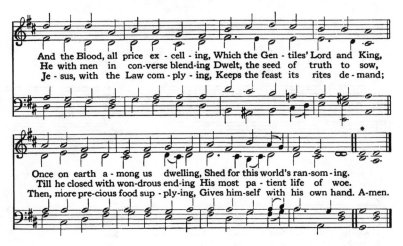

And the Blood, all price ex - cell - ing, Which the Gen - tiles' Lord and King,
He with men in con-verse blend-ing Dwelt, the seed of truth to sow,
Je - sus, with the Law com - ply - ing, Keeps the feast its rites de - mand;

Once on earth a - mong us dwelling, Shed for this world's ran-som-ing.
Till he closed with won-drous end-ing His most pa - tient life of woe.
Then, more pre-cious food sup - ply-ing, Gives him-self with his own hand. A-men.

Example 4
Now, My Tongue, the Mystery Telling
Accompaniment © 1984, Jackson Hill. Used by permission.

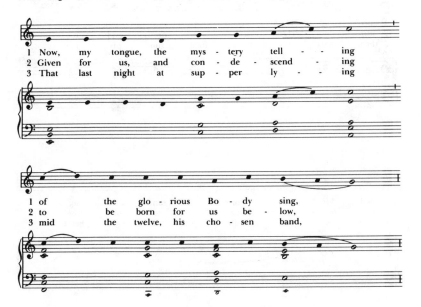

1 Now, my tongue, the mys - tery tell - - ing
2 Given for us, and con - de - scend - ing
3 That last night at sup - per ly - - ing

1 of the glo - rious Bo - dy sing,
2 to be born for us be - low,
3 mid the twelve, his cho - sen band,

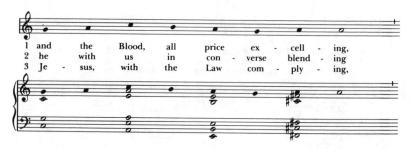

1 and the Blood, all price ex - cell - ing,
2 he with us in con - verse blend - ing
3 Je - sus, with the Law com - ply - ing,

1 which the Gen - tiles' Lord and King,
2 dwelt, the seed of truth to sow,
3 keeps the feast its rites de - mand;

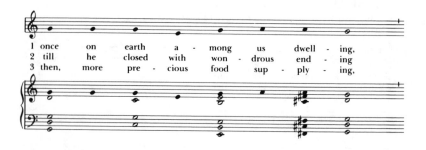

1 once on earth a - mong us dwell - ing,
2 till he closed with won - drous end - ing
3 then, more pre - cious food sup - ply - ing,

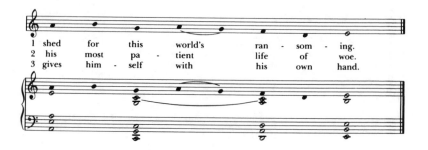

1 shed for this world's ran - som - ing.
2 his most pa - tient life of woe.
3 gives him - self with his own hand.

Example 5
How Firm a Foundation

"K" in Rippon's *Selection*, 1787   Early American Melody

1 How firm a foun - da - tion, ye saints of the Lord,
2 "Fear not, I am with thee; O be not dis - mayed,
3 "When through fier - y tri - als thy path - way shall lie,
4 "The soul that on Je - sus hath leaned for re - pose

1 Is laid for your faith in His ex - cel - lent Word!
2 For I am thy God, and will still give thee aid;
3 My grace, all suf - fi - cient, shall be thy sup - ply:
4 I will not, I will not de - sert to its foes;

1 What more can He say than to you He hath said,
2 I'll strength - en thee, help thee, and cause thee to stand,
3 The flame shall not hurt thee; I on - ly de - sign
4 That soul, though all hell should en - deav - or to shake,

1 To you who for ref - uge to Je - sus have fled?
2 Up - held by My right - eous, om - nip - o - tent hand.
3 Thy dross to con - sume and thy gold to re - fine.
4 I'll nev - er, no nev - er, no nev - er for - sake!"

Example 6
How Firm a Foundation

Example 7
A Mighty Fortress Is Our God
From *The Hymnal 1982*, © Church Pension Fund. Used by permission.

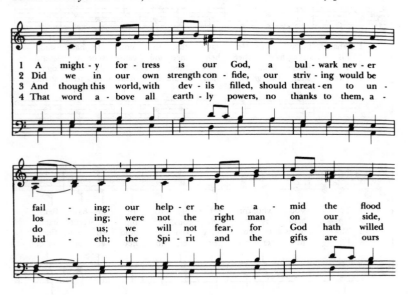

of mor - tal ills pre - vail - ing: for still our an - cient foe
the man of God's own choos - ing: dost ask who that may be?
his truth to tri - umph through us; the prince of dark - ness grim,
through him who with us sid - eth: let goods and kin - dred go,

doth seek to work us woe; his craft and power are great,
Christ Je - sus, it is he; Lord Sa - ba - oth his Name,
we trem - ble not for him; his rage we can en - dure,
this mor - tal life al - so; the bo - dy they may kill:

and, armed with cru - el hate, on earth is not his e - qual.
from age to age the same, and he must win the bat - tle.
for lo! his doom is sure, one lit - tle word shall fell him.
God's truth a - bid - eth still, his king - dom is for ev - er.

Words: Martin Luther (1483-1546); tr. Frederick Henry Hedge (1805-1890); based on Psalm 46
Music: *Ein feste Burg*, melody Martin Luther (1483-1546);
   harm. Johann Sebastian Bach (1685-1750)   87. 87. 66. 66. 7

Example 8
A Mighty Fortress Is Our God
From *The Hymnal 1982*, © Church Pension Fund. Used by permission.

1 A might - y for - tress is our God, a bul - wark
2 Did we in our own strength con - fide, our striv - ing
3 And though this world, with dev - ils filled, should threat - en
4 That word a - bove all earth - ly powers, no thanks to

nev-er fail - ing;   our help-er he a-mid the flood
would be los - ing;   were not the right man on our side,
to un-do us;   we will not fear, for God hath willed
them, a-bid - eth;   the Spi-rit and the gifts are ours

of mor-tal ills pre-vail - ing: for still our an-cient foe
the man of God's own choos - ing: dost ask who that may be?
his truth to tri-umph through us;   the prince of dark-ness grim,
through him who with us sid - eth: let goods and kin-dred go,

doth seek to work us woe; his craft and power are great,
Christ Je-sus, it is he; Lord Sa-ba-oth his Name,
we trem-ble not for him; his rage we can en-dure,
this mor-tal life al-so; the bo-dy they may kill:

and, armed with cru-el hate, on earth is not his e - - qual.
from age to age the same, and he must win the bat - - tle.
for lo! his doom is sure, one lit-tle word shall fell him.
God's truth a-bid-eth still, his king-dom is for ev - - er.

Alternative tune: *Ein feste Burg* (isometric), 688.

Words: Martin Luther (1483-1546); tr. Frederic Henry Hedge (1805-1890); based on Psalm 46
Music: *Ein feste Burg*, melody Martin Luther (1483;1546);
     harm. Hans Leo Hassler (1564-1612), alt.

♩=100

87. 87. 66. 66. 7

Example 9
Come, We That Love the Lord

1. Come, we that love the Lord, And let our joys be known,
2. Let those re - fuse to sing Who nev - er knew our God,
3. The hill of Zi - on yields A thou - sand sa - cred sweets
4. Then let our songs a - bound And ev - ery tear be dry;

Join in a song with sweet ac-cord, Join in a song with sweet ac-cord
But chil-dren of the heav'n-ly King, But chil-dren of the heav'n-ly King
Be - fore we reach the heav'n-ly fields, Be - fore we reach the heav'n-ly fields
We're march-ing thro' Im-manuel's ground, We're march-ing thro' Im-man-uel's ground

And thus sur - round the throne, And thus sur-round the throne.
May speak their joys a - broad, May speak their joys a - broad.
Or walk the gold - en streets, Or walk the gold - en streets.
To fair - er worlds on high, To fair - er worlds on high.

Refrain

We're march-ing to *Zi - on, Beau-ti-ful, beau-ti-ful Zi - on;

We're march-ing up-ward to Zi - on, The beau-ti-ful cit-y of God.

TEXT: Isaac Watts; Robert Lowry, Refrain   MARCHING TO ZION
MUSIC: Robert Lowry   6.6.8.8.6.6. with Refrain

*Psalm 2:6. By extension this refers to the New Jerusalem.

Example 10
Come, We That Love the Lord

1. Come, we that love the Lord, And let our joys be known; Join
2. Let those re - fuse to sing Who nev - er knew our God; But
3. The men of grace have found Glo - ry be - gun be - low; Ce -
4. The hill of Zi - on yields A thou - sand sa - cred sweets Be -
5. Then let our songs a - bound, And ev - ery tear be dry; We're

in   a song with sweet ac - cord, And thus sur - round the throne.
chil - dren of the heav'n-ly King May speak their joys a - broad.
les - tial fruit on earth - ly ground From faith and hope may grow.
fore we reach the heav'n-ly fields, Or walk the gold - en streets.
march-ing thro' Em - man - uel's ground To fair - er worlds on high. A - men.

TEXT: Isaac Watts   ST. THOMAS
MUSIC: Aaron Williams   S.M.

Example 11
Jesus, I Come

William T. Sleeper, 1819 - 1904   George C. Stebbins, 1846 - 1945

1. Out of my bond- age, sor-row and night, Je-sus, I come, Je-sus, I come;
2. Out of my shame-ful fail -ure and loss, Je-sus, I come, Je-sus, I come;
3. Out of un - rest and ar - ro-gant pride, Je-sus, I come, Je-sus, I come;
4. Out of the fear and dread of the tomb, Je-sus, I come, Je-sus, I come;

Into Thy free-dom, glad-ness and light, Je-sus, I come to Thee;
Into the glo-rious gain of Thy cross, Je-sus, I come to Thee;
Into Thy bless-ed will to a-bide, Je-sus, I come to Thee;
Into the joy and light of Thy home, Je-sus, I come to Thee;

Out of my sick-ness in-to Thy health, Out of my want and in-to Thy wealth,
Out of earth's sor-rows in-to Thy balm, Out of life's storms and in-to Thy calm,
Out of my-self to dwell in Thy love, Out of de-spair in-to rap-tures a-bove,
Out of the depths of ru-in un-told, In-to the peace of Thy shel-ter-ing fold,

Out of my sin and in-to Thy-self, Je-sus, I come to Thee.
Out of dis-tress to ju-bi-lant psalm, Je-sus, I come to Thee.
Up-ward for aye on wings like a dove, Je-sus, I come to Thee.
Ev-er Thy glo-rious face to be-hold, Je-sus, I come to Thee.

Example 12
O Little Town of Bethlehem
From *The Hymnal 1982*, © Church Pension Fund. Used by permission.

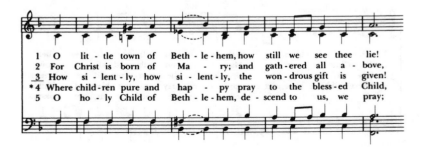

1 O lit-tle town of Beth-le-hem, how still we see thee lie!
2 For Christ is born of Ma-ry; and gath-ered all a-bove,
3 How si-lent-ly, how si-lent-ly, the won-drous gift is given!
*4 Where child-ren pure and hap-py pray to the bless-ed Child,
5 O ho-ly Child of Beth-le-hem, de-scend to us, we pray;

1 A - bove thy deep and dream-less sleep the si - lent stars go by;
2 while mor-tals sleep, the an - gels keep their watch of won-dering love.
<u>3</u> So God im-parts to hu - man hearts the bless-ings of his heaven.
4 where mis-er - y cries out to thee, Son of the mo - ther mild;
5 cast out our sin and en - ter in, be born in us to - day.

1 yet in thy dark streets shin - eth the ev - er - last - ing Light;
2 O morn-ing stars, to - geth - er pro - claim the ho - ly birth!
<u>3</u> No ear may hear his com - ing, but in this world of sin,
4 where char - i - ty stands watch-ing and faith holds wide the door,
5 We hear the Christ-mas an - gels the great glad tid - ings tell;

1 the hopes and fears of all the years are met in thee to - night.
2 and prais - es sing to God the King, and peace to men on earth.
<u>3</u> where meek souls will re - ceive him, still the dear Christ en - ters in.
4 the dark night wakes, the glo - ry breaks, and Christ - mas comes once more.
5 O come to us, a - bide with us, our Lord Em - man - u - el!

Words: Phillips Brooks (1835-1893)
Music: *St. Louis*, Lewis H. Redner (1831-1908)   CMD

Example 13
O Little Town of Bethlehem
From *The Hymnal 1982*, © Church Pension Fund. Used by permission.

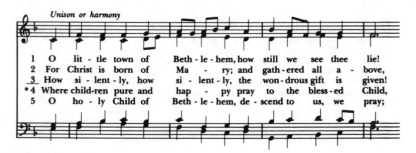

Unison or harmony

1 O lit - tle town of Beth - le - hem, how still we see thee lie!
2 For Christ is born of Ma - ry; and gath - ered all a - bove,
<u>3</u> How si - lent - ly, how si - lent - ly, the won - drous gift is given!
* 4 Where child-ren pure and hap - py pray to the bless - ed Child,
5 O ho - ly Child of Beth - le - hem, de - scend to us, we pray;

1 A - bove thy deep and dream-less sleep the si - lent stars go by;
2 while mor-tals sleep, the an - gels keep their watch of won-dering love.
3 So God im-parts to hu - man hearts the bless-ings of his heaven.
4 where mis - er - y cries out to thee, Son of the mo - ther mild;
5 cast out our sin and en - ter in, be born in us to - day.

1 yet in thy dark streets shin - eth the ev - er - last - ing Light;
2 O morn-ing stars, to - geth - er pro - claim the ho - ly birth!
3 No ear may hear his com - ing, but in this world of sin,
4 where char - i - ty stands watch - ing and faith holds wide the door,
5 We hear the Christ-mas an - gels the great glad tid - ings tell;

1 the hopes and fears of all the years are met in thee to - night.
2 and prais - es sing to God the King, and peace to men on earth.
3 where meek souls will re - ceive him, still the dear Christ en - ters in.
4 the dark night wakes, the glo - ry breaks, and Christ-mas comes once more.
5 O come to us, a - bide with us, our Lord Em - man - u - el!

Words: Philips Brooks (1835-1893)
Music: *Forest Green*, English melody; adapt. and harm. Ralph Vaughan Williams (1872-1958)   CMD

Example 14
Oh, Believe It
From *Hymns of Truth and Praise*, © Truth and Praise, Inc. Used by permission.

John Ferguson, 1864-1940   James R. Murray, 1841-1905

1. There's a sto - ry ev - er new, It is won-der-ful and true, And the
2. I was serv - ing Sa - tan well, And in sin did far ex - cel, And would
3. Then I lis-tened and He said, It was just for you I bled, And with
4. I could then with-stand no more, For I saw my sins, He bore, So I

best thing you can do, Is be-lieve it: It will calm your trou-bled breast,
soon have been in hell; I be-lieve it: But the Sav-iour, He drew near,
me He sweet-ly pled, To be-lieve it: This is now sal - va-tion's day,
en - tered by the door, And be-lieved it: Now I'm hap - py all the day,

And will give you peace and rest, It's of all the news the best,
And He stopped my mad ca - reer, And He told me nev - er fear,
Sin has all been put a - way, This is what I heard Him say,
I can sing as well as pray, For my sins are washed a - way,

REFRAIN

Oh, be - lieve it!
Just be - lieve it!   Oh, be - lieve it!   Oh, be - lieve it! Christ has
Oh, be - lieve it!
I be - lieve it!

died up - on the tree, That from sin you might be free; Oh, be - lieve it!

Oh, be - lieve it!   Je - sus died for you and me,   Oh, be - lieve it!

Example 15
Must I Go and Empty Handed?

Example 16
Dorian Mode

Example 17
Phrygian Mode

Example 18
O Blest Creator, Source of Light
Hypomixolydian Mode (transposed)
From *The Hymnal 1982*, © Church Pension Fund. Used by permission.

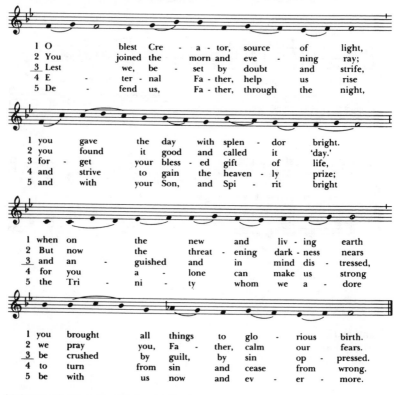

1 O		blest	Cre -	a - tor,	source	of	light,
2 You		joined the		morn and	eve -	ning	ray;
3 Lest		we, be -		set by	doubt	and	strife,
4 E -		ter - nal		Fa - ther,	help	us	rise
5 De -		fend us,		Fa - ther,	through	the	night,

1 you	gave	the	day	with	splen -	dor	bright.
2 you	found	it	good	and	called	it	'day.'
3 for -	get	your	bless -	ed	gift	of	life,
4 and	strive	to	gain	the	heaven -	ly	prize;
5 and	with	your	Son,	and	Spi -	rit	bright

1 when	on	the	new	and	liv -	ing	earth
2 But	now	the	threat -	ening	dark -	ness	nears
3 and	an -	guished	and	in	mind	dis -	tressed,
4 for	you	a -	lone	can	make	us	strong
5 the	Tri -	ni -	ty	whom	we	a -	dore

1 you	brought	all	things	to	glo -	rious	birth.
2 we	pray	you,	Fa -	ther,	calm	our	fears.
3 be	crushed	by	guilt,	by	sin	op -	pressed,
4 to	turn	from	sin	and	cease	from	wrong.
5 be	with	us	now	and	ev -	er -	more.

Words: Latin, 6th cent.; tr. Anne K. LeCroy (b. 1930), alt.
Music: *Lucis creator optime*, plainsong, Mode 8, Verona MS., 11th cent.   LM

Example 19
All Glory, Laud, and Honor, 10th century version
Dorian Mode
Copyright © 1984, Schola Antiqua Inc., La Casa del Libro, San Juan,
Puerto Rica 00901. Used by permission.

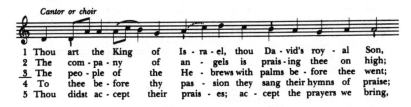

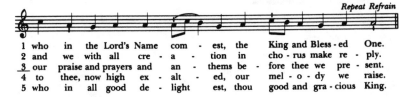

Words: Theodulph of Orleans (d. 821); tr. John Mason Neale (1818-1866), alt.
Music: *Gloria, laus, et honor*, plainsong, Mode 1, Einsiedeln MS. and St. Gall MS., 10th cent.;
    ver. Schola Antiqua, 1983   76. 76 with Refrain

Example 20
All Glory Laud and Honor, chorale version, C major
From *The Hymnal 1982*, © Church Pension Fund. Used by permission.

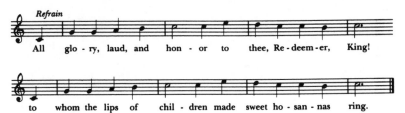

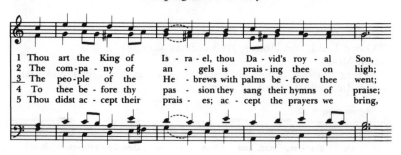

1 Thou art the King of Is - ra - el, thou Da - vid's roy - al Son,
2 The com - pa - ny of an - gels is prais - ing thee on high;
3 The peo - ple of the He - brews with palms be - fore thee went;
4 To thee be - fore thy pas - sion they sang their hymns of praise;
5 Thou didst ac - cept their prais - es; ac - cept the prayers we bring,

Repeat Refrain

1 who in the Lord's Name com - est, the King and Bless - ed One.
2 and we with all cre - a - tion in cho - rus make re - ply.
3 our praise and prayers and an - thems be - fore thee we pre - sent.
4 to thee, now high ex - alt - ed, our mel - o - dy we raise.
5 who in all good de - light - est, thou good and gra - cious King.

The stanzas may be sung by choir alone or alternately by contrasted groups; all sing the refrain.

Words: Theodulph of Orleans (d. 821); tr. John Mason Neale (1818-1866), alt.
Music: *Valet will ich dir geben,* melody Melchior Teschner (1584-1635), alt.;
   harm. Wiliam Henry Monk (1823-1889)   76. 76. D

Example 21
Example of monotonic recitation
from Psalm 141:2.

Let my prayer be set before thee as in - cense.

Notes

1. *Lutheran Book of Worship* (Minneapolis, Minn.: Augsburg Publishing House, 1978), 228.

2. Deryck Cooke, *The Language of Music* (London: Oxford University, 1962), 54.

3. See Eric Werner, *The Sacred Bridge* (New York: Columbia University, 1959). It is Werner's contention that definite musical links exist between ancient Judaism and Christianity. The newly emerging Christian church appropriated many of the musical principles and practices, as well as much of the music, of the Jewish faith. Also see A. Z. Idelsohn, *Jewish Music* (New York: Schocken Books, 1967). Also Suzanne Haik-Vantoura, *The Music of the Bible Revealed*, translated from the French by Dennis Weber and John Wheeler (Berkeley, Calif.: BIBAL Press, 1991), 140.

4. Joseph Sittler, "Provocations on the Church and the Arts," *The Christian Century*, 19–26 March 1986, 293.

5. Virgil Thomson, "Ethical Content," *The Art of Judging Music* (Westport, Conn.: Greenwood, 1948), 302.

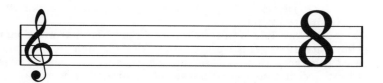

Church Music as Gospel Analogue

Symbols

The Need for Symbols

Human beings alone have the capacity and the need to live by symbols. Our need to objectify whole levels of experience, past and present, makes us symbol-making creatures. People intuitively encode in symbols the most meaningful events of their lives. A wedding ring, for example, symbolizes not only a wedding ceremony, but wedded life and marriage as an institution. The meaning of a ring obviously supersedes its physical attributes.

Human history, the repository of our identity, is laced with symbols. Without them we would not be able to manage the complex reality which defines us as people. The flag, cross, or swastika impart an instant meaning behind the symbol, representing all that is past and giving the present a direction for the future. Symbols are objects, sounds, or actions which depict something else, having the power to bring to us that which is represented and to stir us to further action. Symbols evoke and provoke.

Symbol as Metaphor

A symbol is a metaphor. That is, it uses the familiar to communicate and open up new depths of comprehension. In ancient Israel trees did not literally clap their hands and brooks did not sing. But trees which "clap their hands" and brooks which "sing," metaphorically give to us an understanding of nature praising God from the psalmist's point of view. Loosely speaking, the incarnate Christ himself was the ultimate metaphor! Jesus became man. He took on human form so God could communicate with us, opening levels of understanding not possible any other way. Things of our world, water, fire, bread, and oil, are used to tell us about his world and as symbols help bridge the gap between God and humans. We understand the divine in terms of the temporal. Water reflects God's internal cleansing and purification; a lamb signifies Christ's place in the act of redemption; and the dove suggests purity and peace. In addition, ritual acts of the church, such as baptism and holy communion, are metaphors: outward and visible symbols of an inward and spiritual grace.

Music too is a metaphor, speaking symbolically and generating meaning beyond itself on different levels simultaneously. One level would be emotion: joy, sorrow, longing. Another is beauty: grace, elegance, form. Moreover, it may open up levels of meaning commensurate with language such as that found in program music. Here musical motifs and themes represent story characters. The interplay of themes tells the story. Music can call us to arms, bring about patriotic fervor, or cause nostalgia for one's alma mater. Being bound to the stuff of our world, symbols are grounded in the tangible. Music, however, also offers realms that go beyond the temporal to the transcendent, to levels of reality which touch upon the ultimate questions of life.

Church Music as Gospel Analogue

Church music is a symbol. It is an analogue of the gospel, a musical witness to gospel meaning. It not only passively represents the numinous but actively works out gospel principles in notes, rhythm, and harmony, constituting a musical show-and-tell of the gospel. No doubt very few have ever thought about it in this way, for church music is usually believed to be passively neutral. Nevertheless, music always gives off a theological witness which is assimilated unconsciously or consciously. Whether we desire it or not, church music as gospel analogue always makes a statement of some kind. The power of music to symbolically represent the gospel is an important consideration when developing a discipling ministry of music.

The big question is not, "Does music witness?" but, "What will be the content of our musical witness?" One should not take for granted that church music is always a positive affirmation of the faith. Some sets of musical symbols (i.e., pieces of church music) are much better and truer in representing the faith than others. The director's job is to be sure that the music of a discipling ministry represents in its grammar the implications of the church's theology. Music must be influenced in its melody, harmony, rhythms, colors, and instrumentation by the practical application of theology. The gospel's penchant for the narrow way, the hard way, and the disciplined way, shows the need for a music which analogically and symbolically expresses these things. Integrity, truth, creativity, purity, economy, and self-denial rather than the traits of showmanship, pleasure, banality, cheapness, and amusement are suitable to church music. And yet these latter are often the ones actually operative in much of the church's music! Just as a Christian whose deeds and actions do not measure up to gospel requirements brings disrepute on the gospel, so poor music does the same thing.

Analogue of the Spirit of Our Age

Suggesting that the Christian faith can be translated into musical/gospel symbolism is for many people a completely new way of apprehending church music. Getting beyond the notes and finding the meanings which they represent shows that some church music has often been more of an analogue of the world than of the gospel.

Church music has taken up an analogical relationship with nontheistic worldviews because congregations, pastors, and musicians have not been careful in evaluating our music, culture, church culture, and the relationships between them. Usually our sights have been set on making church music comfortable and pleasing—that is, popular. In a culture with a general disregard for the highest musical quality, achieving popularity has meant sacrificing integrity. Sometimes this was done purposefully, as is exemplified in the music after the Second Vatican Council, much of which has been largely world-affirming. Certain branches of

Protestantism also designed programs for pleasuring the tastes of people, resulting in a lowered compositional quality. When music is believed to be theologically neutral, there is no compulsion to use the best music. Instead, our attention is riveted to making church music please the self at any cost.

Some Concerns of a Discipling Ministry of Music

The Incarnation—Limited Accommodation

There is a side to the gospel which is partially accommodative to culture. If the gospel is anything at all, it is incarnational. The divine came in human form. Music which mirrors theology as an analogue of gospel meaning operates in the tension between the human and the divine. To be incarnational means music cannot be so unintelligible that it is totally incomprehensible. Nor should it be so world-affirming that it functions as unabashed entertainment. We have a tightrope to walk, a counterpoint to establish, a balance to achieve.

Church music ought to be a symbolic picture of God's relationship with his children, a musical analogy of heaven coming to earth and earth being possessed and directed by heaven. The best way to describe the procedure is for us to see the event of the God-man as a counterpoint between the earthly and the heavenly. The process of doing church music then becomes a contrapuntal process in which the heavenly is made understandable to the earthly, and the earthly is raised to the heavenly. Music as gospel analogue, then, must not only be disciplined by gospel traits, but also take into concern the ability of people to interpret the musical symbol correctly. This is not as difficult as it might seem. Within our Western culture there is a general musical understanding, albeit a very basic one common to all people. True, each group will have somewhat different expressions, but within these musical expressions will be those most suitable for gospel witness.

Adaptation to culture is a necessary part of music's analogically being the gospel. If we believe the gospel is for everyone, then choice of music needs to be based, in part, upon that which is comprehensible to people. Hence, church music needs to be an invitation with enough openness for it to be meaningful to the ordinary hearer. It does no good if the music of a discipling ministry is unrelated to people's circumstances. The key here is to have the wisdom to know when the witness of church music has become garbled. In other words, the real danger is not that church music becomes so heavenly minded that it is no earthly good, but conversely that it becomes too worldly minded to be of any heavenly good. Usually congregations want music which amuses them or proves to be emotionalistic. This goes too far in accommodation. Music which does not amuse people is not necessarily alien to them.

That churchgoers naturally assume culture's stance in matters pertaining to musical hedonism indicates a distinct need for a music program which attempts to correct such understanding. It is critical. Music as gospel analogue must symbolically accommodate culture only to a limited extent. That is, musical hedonism which strips the gospel of its disciplining principles must be avoided. If there is a question, church music should err on the side of musical discipline.

Music can be accommodating without being the assembly's favorite popular music. The issue is its being understandable, not its being likable. Incarnational accommodation does not automatically mean gospel pop.

Integrity

The church must utilize music with depth. Symbols that lack depth lack integrity. Church music which has the depth to take on gospel meaning metaphorically must be wholesome, free of carnal associations, and have the attributes and quality of good art. Its creativity, delayed gratification, and aesthetic truth provide the characteristics necessary for symbolically representing the Christian faith. Shallowness, novelty, or banality lack the necessary standards and only bring disrepute on the gospel.

Community Symbols

Musical symbols must be community symbols. That is to say, they must be assimilable by the people as a whole. Privatization fails to do justice to the corporate nature of the body of Christ. This poses a dilemma, since people come from all walks of life, educational backgrounds, and socio-economic classes, and they vary in musical abilities, levels of spiritual maturity, and artistic inclinations. Is it possible that musical symbols can be found for such a diverse group? Yes. The universality of musical language assures us that church music of integrity can be comprehended rationally and emotionally by everyone. We accommodate the assembly by determining their average musical/spiritual center and by using music within those parameters insofar as they are faithful to gospel witness.

Teaching

If musical symbols are to be understood in a common context, the best way we have of achieving that goal in such a diverse culture is to instruct the faithful in the symbolic meanings of church music. Two things happen when teaching becomes a high priority. First, people move closer; they develop a shared musical expression of the faith. Second, musicians can better exercise a prophetic ministry in shepherding the congregation toward discipleship. When the assembly understands that there is more to church music than just setting texts to favorite music, a discipling program can be implemented in which congregation, pastor, and musician all work together for a common good—the maturing of the saints. Biblically disciplined church music, that which is a faithful analogy of the gospel, needs careful nurture within the community of the faithful.

The Directional Balance of Pastoral Music Ministry

Pastoral music ministry is aware of the tension between the world and heaven, and it champions a direction in which ministry has one foot in the worldly realm and the other firmly in the heavenly. It affirms people by helping them become more and more like the perfect image of God. Pastoral ministry always does what is best for people, not what simply affirms their earthbound fleshly desires. When we take into account the ultimate well-being of our people, the musical symbols we use must be characterized (within cultural bounds) by the sterling qualities of the gospel itself.

For church music to be a full musical analogue of the gospel, then, requires a discipled approach to church music making which is pastoral in the full sense of the word. We become aware of where we are, where we should be, and then point our ministry in the direction we should move.

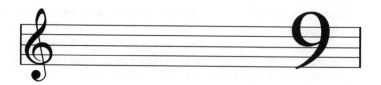

Directions for the Twenty-first Century

Practics—Congregations, Pastors, and Musicians

Congregational Involvement

The more church members are actively involved in the music of the church, the more receptive they will be to the discipling aspects of music ministry. To that end directors of music need open lines of communication with their congregations on matters of mutual concern. Such dialogue can be informal or formal. But whatever the setting, welcoming their thoughts, suggestions, criticisms, and inquiries will go far in establishing the kind of rapport necessary for making music ministry as effective as possible in any given situation.

One of the ways dialogue can be enhanced is the formation of a representative music council or committee of some kind. When its purpose is task-oriented rather than policy-oriented, such a commission can be very helpful. That is, a group of people who share ideas and carry out assigned duties assist more effectively than a committee designed to legislate musical policy. As a matter of fact, a policy-making body is apt to have a

negative effect on music ministry because directors need freedom of action to do their work well. Prophetic ministry is
severely limited by rigid democratic procedure. People who are
in need of ministry often do not have the capability of knowing
what is best for them. Telephoning, typing letters, car-pooling,
making punch and cookies, repairing vestments, and doing library work are more valuable than their setting a cap on the
volume level of the organ prelude, for example, or choosing the
hymns for the next three months. Mostly, directors need extra
help. The music minister who has a committee which assists on
a regular basis is extremely fortunate.

Congregations, as the object of music ministry, may also
be involved in the program through a systematic teaching program. At some point the assembly needs to become aware of the
larger goal, scope, and methods of music ministry. There are
many possibilities for such a forum: a church school class for a
certain unit of time; mid-week services; a few minutes prior to
Sunday morning worship (this would be a good place for a
congregational rehearsal); occasional instruction during the sermon or announcement time; or inserts in the Sunday bulletin. It
might be possible to have the music director spend a unit of
time—four or more sessions—with informal house groups to
share the goals and methodology of music in the parish. Every
inquirer's class, confirmation class, and church membership class
should have some sessions devoted to the ministry of music.
These should be teaching sessions, not just presentations of
"opportunities for service." The severe cleavage between our
general pop musical culture and a biblical program of church
music demands that teaching on music ministry be a normal
topic of study for those who are taking upon themselves the vows
of church membership. Unless this is done, it is difficult to
achieve congregational progress, because newcomers are not
properly acclimated to the goals and methodology of music
ministry. They will tend therefore to slow down the progress of
the congregation as a whole.

Pastoral Understanding and Support

Pastors who pragmatically use music in their ministry are
seldom concerned with music as gospel analogue or as holistic
maturing agent. They are concerned with externals: the as-

sembly's enjoyment, music as a drawing card, musical recreation, and worship manipulation. In such situations there is little music can contribute to the maturing of God's saints.

The tremendous importance of a discipling music ministry within the context of the overall church program must be clearly understood by the pastor if it is to be most effective. It would seem logical that once the goal of music ministry was explained, clergy would welcome it as another help in developing parish life in God. And in truth, most pastors do welcome it.

But many clergy who are quick to affirm the general aims of such a ministry often do not understand its implementation. They get bogged down in details: should we sing this hymn, or that hymn, or no hymn at all? Should choir anthems be given a place of importance in the service or be incidental and used as "filler"? Are choruses to be sung, and if so, which ones, when, and how many times each? Should oratorios, cantatas, or "musicales" be of the "pop" music type or the "classic" type and when, if they are to be used, should they be presented? What items of the service should be sung—psalms, prayers, the ordinary of the Mass (such as the Gloria, Creed, or Sanctus), acclamations, opening sentences, versicles, and benedictions—and what music should be used for each? What ought be the general style of the music? Is silence or background music to be used? Deciding these particulars tends to cause problems between pastors and musicians. It would be much better for pastors to trust their musicians' judgments in such technical details, offering instead general guidelines, psychological support, and spiritual encouragement. Respectful dialogue is more productive than a continual tug of war. When pastor and staff share ministry, they demonstrate a model from which the congregation can pattern their own use of gifts. In the long run, a responsible collaborative ministry is the most productive approach.

Musicians—Technique and Spirituality

The musician who is to exercise a full-orbed ministry must be both technically proficient and spiritually aware. Excellence as a keyboardist, vocalist, or conductor does not insure that ministry will be everything that it should be; nor does spiritual sensitivity without excellence in technique have the capability of addressing spiritual concerns through the highly technical language of music. Musicians tend to favor one or the other. Some are interested in the excellence of the music, wanting to play, sing, and conduct only the best music. Some musicians, though, more interested in the "message" getting across, tend to place less emphasis on the craft of singing, playing, conducting, or composing. Either type of one-sidedness is unsatisfactory.

The plea here is for musicians to emphasize both technique and spirituality. After all, these are not mutually exclusive. Those who are naturally concerned with technique first and foremost, should become aware of the spiritual dimensions of music in parish life. Those who are spiritually aware need to recognize that a poor medium (quality of musical composition and execution) degrades the message. In clarifying their goals, and understanding the how, what, and why of achieving them, musicians will be acutely concerned for both the technical and the spiritual.

Musicians—Administration

Organization is essential to effectively managing a discipling music ministry. When goals and methods are marshalled into a working structure based upon the resources of the parish, a beginning can be made. Of course the individual local church situation will make a great deal of difference in the details of implementing a music ministry. But the following general organizational guidelines may be helpful.

A three-pronged approach to overseeing the music program of a parish works well for most directors. Such a structure gives clarity to the process of administration. First, as we have previously stated, the congregation is the specific target of ministry; second, the choirs, soloists, and instrumental ensembles are the means of ministry; third, the leader(s)—such as the leaders of the children's choirs, bell choirs, orchestra, organists, pianists, music council, the music director, and the pastor—form the management team. Using such a trio (recipients, means, and management) offers a workable organization to the ministry structure. It gives a focus for ministry, a defined means for ministering, and an administrative setup which allows for flexibility, supervision, and accountability. Such a structure will allow the particulars of ministry to develop: definitive congregational goals, the organization of ministering units with the necessary personnel for judicious staffing, and the input necessary for competent decision-making.

Our present study is not intended as a text on music administration, i.e., the making and carrying out of a plan. There are, however, a few specific things which will show how a more discipled approach to music might be implemented.

The overall goal of maturing the saints of God needs a carefully balanced plan to cause the congregation to move forward but not to the point of total disorientation. An example might be the elimination of background music during prayers. For a congregation which has been used to corporate prayer with musical background, a plan to eliminate such inducement may take a number of years. In the first year we may continue it at a greatly reduced volume level; the second, include frequent lapses into silence; and the third, only infrequently include musical background. Perhaps by the end of the third year it could be totally abolished. While some musicians would opt for eliminating it in one grand sweep, a more gradual tapering off is the more practical solution where it has been used extensively. In any case, being able to pray without artificial stimulation goes a long way toward making individual and corporate prayer more disciplined and mature.

The same approach would work for including more disciplined hymns and anthems in the assembly's repertoire. Gradually increasing the number of more mature expressions and little by little eliminating others is an effective method of moving the congregation forward. If the congregation is belligerent about its right to enjoy the romantic grand old gospel favorites of yesteryear or the popular songs of CCM, remedial education must be undertaken to help them. To simply sing a better quality of music instantly is not quite the answer in such situations (many of us wish it were). The skill of a minister of music is shown by his or her ability to cause change without undue dissatisfaction and hostility.

To begin, a director might find one well-known hymn or choir anthem of better quality and use it as a point of departure. For example, almost everyone knows "All Hail the Power of Jesus' Name" (*Coronation*) and the "Hallelujah Chorus" of Georg F. Handel. Find other hymns and anthems of the same style, genre, and quality, and add them to the repertoire. "Alleluia! Sing to Jesus" (*Hyfrydol*) and Handel's "Break Forth Into

Joy" ("Messiah") would be possibilities. Sing the new songs frequently. (More will be said about this later.) They soon will work their way into the hearts of the people. Little by little a more wholesome repertoire could take the place of the shallow favorites congruent with humanistic pop culture.

The organization of recipient, means, and management into a unified structure will help the overall goal of ministry to be achieved in the most efficient and direct way. Matters concerning budget, personnel, philosophy, and methodology can all be dealt with in relation to the whole. But whatever item we address, we must keep in mind that God's principles are the only ones we can legitimately use. Only they will bear good fruit in years to come. Shortcuts and a pragmatic approach to ministry are dead ends. That which does not stand up to scripture ought not be part of our modus operandi. We can lose the war (maturing God's saints) by winning a battle or two using unscrupulous means. Honesty and integrity must be our norms as leaders of the music of God's people.

The Choir

One of the means of ministry, perhaps the main one, is the choir. Through it the director does much of the work of ministry. The actual duties of the choir go far beyond those normally associated with such an ensemble. Though congregational in makeup, it is ministerial in function. The choir ought be a visible microcosm of God's dealings with the whole church, a channel of his grace and glory, and a corporate respondent in the call to holy living and fuller commitment.

The Old Testament documents a well-organized plan for worship leadership. The choir, members of the tribe of Levi, were consecrated and set aside to be part of that leadership, and they were supported in that task by the other eleven tribes. The clerical role of the choir is a biblically corroborated practice that is still needed today.

Responsibilities of the Choir

The following list of pastoral responsibilities shows the priorities which should govern the choir's ministry. It is not exhaustive or inflexible, since each church will have a somewhat different approach depending upon denomination, size, and particular vision of its leadership.

1. To maintain a right attitude toward God, congregation, pastor, music, and musicians.
2. To support the pastor and staff in prayer, word, and deed.
3. To enter into worship wholeheartedly. An unenthusiastic choir will infect the assembly with the same attitude.
4. To be attentive and responsive to every worship leader, whether lector, soloist, preacher, song leader, or celebrant.
5. To lead in the congregational singing of hymns, psalms, and spiritual songs. Such leadership should be with faces, eyes, and heart, as well as with voices.
6. Service music, such as calls to worship, acclamations, benedictions, versicles, and responses, should be sung with vigor and enthusiasm. Music which is repeated from week to week needs special attention, since it may tend to lose freshness.
7. To be helpful in giving prayers, witness, words of edification, or scriptural admonitions, especially when a general invitation has been given without any ready congregational response. The choir should act as icebreaker and prompter.
8. To open up personally to the preached word. Nothing will aid a pastor's sermonic communication more than the example of a choir paying close attention to every word. The assembly will tend to imitate the listeners they see before them. A choir of disinterested, unenthusiastic, unresponsive, sleepy individuals, who feel that because they have finished their "special music" they have no further responsibility, however, grossly misses the point of its ministry. In such a case it would be better to do away with the choir.
9. To give prayer support at the altar to those who respond to any invitation which might be given by the pastor. It is disconcerting when the choir is oblivious to the Spirit's working and is in a hurry to leave. Instead the choir must use its influence to help open the congregation to the gentle and unhurried moving of God's Spirit.
10. To sing any anthem material as deemed appropriate for the service.

The choir is a facilitator of worship, a model of breaking out of the temporal and reaching, if only briefly, the heavenly. It ought to exhibit a worship in spirit and in truth which encourages the congregation to do the same. One can readily see that the main function of the choir is to model worship: taking the initiative, inspiring, helping, and leading.

Individuals in the choir must be systematically taught their role. The priorities and attitudes we wish to foster need to become normative. They are best learned as the music director carefully shepherds the choir into maturing patterns of worship leadership and as the director expects each choir member to practice them regularly and well.

The Pastor's Relationship with the Choir

The pastor needs to nurture a collegial relationship with the choir since they are co-workers. The pastor's personal rapport with the choir greatly enhances its sharing of and identification with the pastor's spiritual vision for the parish. It is important that regular times of intercessory prayer be scheduled, especially prior to each service. Praying together nourishes community. Nothing will so inspire the choir to do its best as the esprit de corps generated by a pastor who genuinely cares about them and expects them to shake the rafters of heaven in their quest for the spiritual advancement of the congregation.

Psalms

Musically, the main priority of the choir should be the leading and supporting of congregational singing: psalms, hymns, and spiritual songs, as well as other vocal music such as service music and any choruses which might be included.

The singing of the psalms is a special category of song mentioned by Paul and ought to be one of the normative musics of the church. It is not, however, a type of song that our society readily takes to. With psalms we are concerned with large chunks of text (not the isolated psalm verse often associated with chorus singing) which normally necessitates the use of some type of cantillation. Strangely enough, there are churches which pride themselves on their fidelity to a literal interpretation of scripture, but which seldom take the passages about singing psalms seriously. It was not always so. The Genevan reformation under John Calvin went to the opposite extreme and would not allow anything other than scripture to be sung in the churches. Hymns of "human composure" were, for the most part, banned. Only psalms and canticles (scriptural songs other than psalms), that is, material of "divine composure," were allowed! If we are to be people of the Book and honor the intention of scripture, we really have no choice but to sing psalms.

The first hurdle to get over in singing psalms is the matter of using a reciting note for the bulk of the text. It ought to become a natural mode of musical expression, and this only happens as the technique is routinized. That means practice and familiarization. Churches in the liturgical tradition are accustomed to chant (though this does not mean an automatic affinity for psalm singing). Also, those charismatic churches who engage in "singing in the Spirit" should be receptive to monotonic recitation. But for the remainder, the idea of singing on one note takes some getting used to. The choir can be a big help here. Perhaps an entire year of rehearsals might be set aside before any attempt is made to incorporate cantillation into the worship service. At each weekly rehearsal, for at least four weeks, a short psalm could be sung on a single pitch. Psalm 117, having only two verses, is a good one with which to begin. Another of five verses, such as Psalm 100, could follow. As cantillation becomes familiar, simple psalm tones could be introduced. If careful attention is paid to the details of singing in chant style, and practice is spread out over a large time span, it eventually will become as natural as speech.

Cantillation at its best is intensified speech. The rhythm and pacing of the recitation should be that of the spoken word, rather deliberate, but with inflections and nuances kept as they would be for regular speech. With larger choirs it is best to pace the singing a bit slower and more regular than that of normal speech. Do not accent the unaccented syllables or break after the commas, though a slight lengthening at such places is helpful. If the verse is extremely long, a breath will need to be taken at some point, usually at a comma. Break after periods, semicolons, and colons. Ease into and out of the phrases so that nothing sounds abrupt. Use an average mid-range pitch. Men and women may sing together or alternate verses (antiphonal singing). Occasionally a responsorial arrangement (alternation between soloist and choir) might be used. Since this kind of music is not for aesthetic edification or emotional satisfaction we are freed from the need to "make something happen." This type of music is in a different category, since its purpose is to carry words, giving them a profundity and color they would not ordinarily have.

Once the normality of recitation is established, one of the more fully developed psalm settings may be chosen. There are a great many from which to choose, more than we can deal with here. But to begin, let us consider the Gregorian office antiphonal psalm tones. One useful set of publications utilizing these tones is *Gradual Psalms: Year A, Gradual Psalms: Year B,* and *Gradual Psalms: Year C* compiled by Richard Crocker.[1] Permission is granted to reproduce each psalm setting as needed for congregational use. There are complete instructions in the preface for singing them. The verses may be sung by a soloist, a choir, or the entire congregation. The antiphons (or refrains, as they are called) are sung by the entire assembly and may be accompanied or unaccompanied. The following psalm is shown first as it appears on the printed page (example 22), and then its literal transcription is given (example 23). Compare the two.

A companion volume to *Gradual Psalms* is *The Plainsong Psalter* edited by James Litton.[2] This volume is especially clear in its typesetting and layout. All one hundred fifty psalms are included, arranged in numerical order.

A closely related method to the Gregorian Psalm tones are the Sarum (Salisbury, England) tones which tend to be a bit simpler. These have been set to the psalms with composed antiphons by James E. Barrett in *The Psalmnary: Gradual Psalms for Cantor and Congregation.*[3] There are also clear instructions on psalm singing which are most helpful to directors and singers. Below (example 24) is a reproduction of the page as printed in Barrett's book. A complete transcription of the same follows (example 25).

A plain type of psalm setting, but one that can be sung in four parts, is simplified Anglican chant. The music may be found in the accompaniment edition, volume 1 of *The Hymnal 1982: Service Music.*[4] The text is sung on the reciting note(s), SATB, until the line's last accented syllable, which is sung on the cadence notes. The format of the tune and text is usually printed as follows (example 26). Below is the performance transcription (example 27).

Regular Anglican chant is another possibility. Single chant uses one verse of the psalm before repeating the chant music. Double chant is twice as long so that two verses are completed before beginning the music over again. This type of chanting is more difficult. It is chorally conceived and often best sung by the choir. A good source book is *The Anglican Chant Psalter*, edited by Alec Wyton.[5] See examples 28 and 29.

One of the most compelling recent developments in psalm singing is the claim by French music theorist Suzanne Haik-Vantoura to have discovered the original music of the Bible. She has transcribed the accents which accompany the words of the Hebrew (Masoretic, ninth cent. A.D.) text into a system of musical notation. The melodies are narrow in range and rather austere.[6] But they are hauntingly beautiful in their contemplative and disciplined way. Many Bible passages, including the Song of Solomon and all one hundred fifty psalms, are available in printed notational form useful for performance by choir or congregation in Hebrew. Recordings are also available, as well as a textbook in English (1991), and articles and a video by John Wheeler concerning Haik-Vantoura's interpretation of the Hebrew accentual markings.[7]

Other types of psalm settings are those developed by Joseph Gelineau[8] and the Taizé community in France.[9] There are also settings available such as *Advent Psalms* by Evertt Frese,[10] *Psalms for Singing* by John Erickson,[11] and *Psalms for the Cantor*, published by World Library Publications, Inc.[12]

Another possibility is metrical psalmody. These settings paraphrase the psalms in rhyme and meter so they may be sung to hymn tunes. Metrical psalmody is not as accurate a translation of the Hebrew as those which use prose. They are possible, however, for the sake of variety. An example is *A New Metrical Psalter* by Christopher L. Webber.[13] See example 30. Note that it is in common meter (86. 86) and can be sung to *Azmon* ("O for a Thousand Tongues to Sing").

If the assembly has a clear understanding of the necessity of psalm singing as evidenced by Old Testament usage, the endorsement of the apostle Paul, our Lord's inclusion of a psalm at the end of the Last Supper, and the practice of the New Testament church, the assembly will take singing them more seriously. Members need to be taught that singing rather than saying the psalms is normal, since that was their intended usage. With a carefully constructed educational program, psalm singing can once more be the powerful congregational song it was intended to be. Determined leadership, congregational openness, and a regular routine of use in worship over a number of years will give the impetus and competency to make the singing of scripture another way of maturing God's saints. If we do not expect this music to be a "music for self-pleasure," but treat it as a biblical musical/spiritual discipline, psalm singing will experience a powerful restoration. When that happens, the ministry of music will have taken a large step toward discipling the people of God.

Hymns

Of psalms, hymns, and spiritual songs, hymn singing is perhaps the most pervasive. But it is also in general decline in many branches of the church, having disappeared altogether in some local congregations. Such disaffection with hymnody is unfortunate. Despite the persistent trends of secular culture, it must be restored to its rightful place if the church is to remain healthy. Hymn singing is mandated by scripture and must not be neglected.

The Scriptural Basis for Hymn Singing

It is not surprising that many hymns are recorded in the Bible, for theological truth is often better served by poetic expression than by propositional declaration. The Bible is filled with art forms.

Hymns were sung regularly by God's people for inspiration, edification, and expressing praise and adoration to God. This assertion is warranted by the more than two hundred explicit references to singing throughout the Bible, by the musical practices of the Jewish people, the New Testament Christians, the early church, and the example of our Lord.

For example, among the more familiar Old Testament hymns is the Song of Moses (Deuteronomy 32). In chapter 31, scripture records that the Lord said to Moses, "Now therefore write ye this song for you, and teach it to the children of Israel." Later in the same chapter we read, "Moses therefore wrote this song the same day, and taught it to the children of Israel." Other Old Testament songs include the "Song of Miriam" (Exodus 15), the Hebraic "*Shema*" (Deuteronomy 6 and Numbers 15), the "Song of Deborah and Barak" (Judges 5), the "Last Words of David" (2 Samuel 23), and the "Song of Hannah" (1 Samuel 2). There are many more.

It is, of course, the Psalms which are the most familiar to us and which take up the most space in scripture. They are a special type of hymn divinely inspired. As the Hebraic hymnal, the psalms were used in temple worship and in the synagogue, having the distinction of being the richest single source of song texts that the church possesses.

We also find many fine examples of hymns in the New Testament. Some, such as the "Song of Mary" ("*Magnificat*," Luke 1:46–55), the "Song of Zacharias" ("*Benedictus Dominus Deus*," Luke 1:68–79), and the "Song of Simeon" ("*Nunc Dimittis*," Luke 2:29–32) are sung on a regular basis in many churches. Others are not as widely known: Romans 15:9, Hebrews 2:6–8, 1 Timothy 3:16, 2 Timothy 2:11–13, and Revelation 5:9, 10.

Because of the large time span it covers, the Old Testament shows a consistent, comprehensive, and well-developed use of the hymnological treasure. The New Testament, however, gives to us only the beginnings of what was to become an exceedingly rich hymnody.

The early Christians fashioned their hymn singing after the Old Testament pattern and the practice of our Lord. Note Jesus' hymn usage at the Last Supper. Matthew 26 and Mark 14 relate that prior to their leaving the Passover meal (a time of divine modeling), Jesus and his disciples sang a hymn. No doubt that hymn was the Hallel Psalms (114–118) traditionally sung at the feast of the Passover.

Three other hymnological references in the New Testament demonstrate the use of hymns in scripture and the New Testament church. The first is a hymn citation by the apostle Paul in Ephesians 5:14. "Therefore it is said: 'Awake, sleeper, and arise from the dead, and Christ shall give you light' " (RSV). Second, Paul continues in verse 19: "addressing one another in psalms and hymns and spiritual songs, singing and making melody to the Lord with all your heart" (RSV). And even more directly in Colossians 3:16 he states, "Let the word of Christ dwell in you richly, as you teach and admonish one another in all wisdom, and as you sing psalms and hymns and spiritual songs" (RSV). Third, Paul reports on the practice of hymn singing in the Corinthian church: "When you meet for worship, each of you contributes a hymn" (1 Cor. 14:26, NEB).

Hymn singing is part of God's plan for his chosen people. We can see in the first example (Eph. 5:14) that God uses hymns in his revelation to us. In the second (Eph. 5:19 and Col. 3:16), Paul instructs us to use hymns ourselves for the praise of God and the edification of the saints. In the third (1 Cor. 14:26), we note the historical fact that the New Testament church did sing hymns as part of their worship.

Technical Characteristics

At the time of Paul's writing, the Greek term "hymn" (*hymnos*) referred to a poem, usually sung in praise of a deity. A study of the extant Greek hymns dedicated to pagan gods helps to illuminate our understanding of the word as Paul knew it. It was a generic term, the emphasis of which was to offer general deference, obeisance, and homage to a god. It often taught some particular factual material concerning the god, or attempted to enlist the deity's support, or challenged the listener to action.

A study of the non-Christian Greek hymns sung in Paul's day shows them to be poetic statements, carefully polished, and well-reasoned. Intellect was stressed. It is this latter orientation, this need for reason, for mind, for understanding, for good form, which is the hymn's distinguishing mark. The hymn is concerned first and foremost with rational content artistically embodied so that its performance would have an emotional impact based on concrete objective worth.

As a well-traveled and well-read scholar, Paul may have heard one of the Greek hymns that has come down to us. At the very least he would have been familiar with the form. We can be sure that under the inspiration and guidance of the Holy Spirit he used the word *hymnos* advisably and knowledgeably in his writing of scripture. Paul wrote to express a specific divine intention.

That intention was to insure that the worshiping community regularly sing music which features the understanding, songs which address the whole person through the mind. Paul's usage of the word referred to songs which showed the depth of the scholar, the creativity of the artist, and the enthusiasm of the zealot. Artistically fashioned rational content was at the heart of the divine intention.

Rationality and Emotionality

For those who tend to discredit hymn singing for whatever reason and prefer to replace hymns with songs such as the increasingly popular choruses and refrains currently in vogue, it would be well to remember Paul's discourse in 1 Corinthians 14. Choruses tend to be musically and textually repetitive, easily learned and memorized. Their emphasis is on emotion, feeling, and sentiment. While hymns may be just as emotional, they are so because of the depth of the text; in contrast, choruses tend to be emotional at the expense of depth. There is an emotionalistic flair to the form which distinguishes it from that of the hymn. In 1 Corinthians 14 Paul sets up an antithesis between emotionality and rationality. The question concerns the use of tongues and the interpretation of tongues. His point is that ecstatic utterances which are not interpreted are of little value in edifying the body. Though emotional, tongues exercised without the rational (the interpretation of tongues in the vernacular) has little to commend it. The emotional is fine—but not without the intellectual. And even then Paul shows his clear bias for rationality over emotionality when he indicates, "In the church I desire to speak five words with my mind that I may instruct others also, rather than ten thousand words in a tongue" (1 Corinthians 14:19, NASB). His preference for the more rational is also shown in his list of musical forms in Ephesians 5:19 and Colossians 3:16. Two forms, psalms and hymns, emphasize the intellect; only one, spiritual songs, emphasizes the emotions. Musical forms, of course, are both emotional and intellectual, but in varying degrees. A balance which features the rational over the irrational is clearly preferred in worship. The more intellectualized hymn should be favored over the more emotionalistic chorus. The hymn's particular balance between reason and emotion makes it unsurpassed as a vehicle for praise, admonition, inspiration, adoration, exhortation, education, and narration.

The Spiritual Merits of Hymns

Some of the hymn's more obvious spiritual benefits are:
1. Hymns bring the intellect into worship in a form which also allows for the emotional.
2. Hymns translate into powerful aesthetic and artistic forms theoretical, doctrinal, and propositional truths.

3. Hymns show the interrelatedness among the theological tenets of the Christian faith.
4. Hymns can systematize the teaching and/or reviewing of the great doctrines of scripture.
5. Hymns allow the worshiping community to recount the story (i.e., the historical aspects of our faith) and often simultaneously point to the messianic age.
6. Good hymns display a comprehensive theological content and have the ability to contextualize specific emphases in relevant language.
7. Good hymns are well-suited to Christian worship because they center on God rather than self.
8. Great hymns show versatility in handling a variety of theological emphases while maintaining the centrality of God as the subject.
9. The hymn is the only congregational musical form which thoroughly and systematically celebrates the cycle of historical biblical events that form the bedrock of our faith.
10. The hymn, as congregational music, requires the exercising of the mental and spiritual disciplines characteristic of maturing Christians.

The greatest contribution hymns make to the church is their fleshing out of biblical material in passionate form. They emphasize content displayed through the feeling tone, urgency, and color of artistic forms. They are a "people's art," a biblical/musical form of the collective people of God. No other form can make such a sweeping claim.

When hymns are sung thoughtfully and enthusiastically one is carried aloft into another realm where truth becomes impassioned. It is as if words alone become inadequate and we are compelled to sing. Biblical content and creative music are an unbeatable combination.

Familiarization Helps

One key to making hymns an accepted musical form is familiarizing people with them. Congregations sing what is familiar, and they are familiar with what they sing. Few would rebel if asked to sing "All Hail the Power of Jesus' Name" (*Coronation*). Yet hymns that have similar poetic and musical content such as "Hail, Thou Once Despised Jesus!" (*In Babilone*) often do not find a ready reception. They are unfamiliar.

The following is a list of practical helps for getting a hymn familiarization program started. It is not exhaustive by any means, and it should not be seen as a rigid "how-to-do-it" routine. The list is only to give general guidance.

1. Chart out a tentative plan, noting the points which follow. As you progress, revise your plan as needed.

2. Include the pastoral staff and members of the congregation in the planning. Their understanding and support will make the process work much better.

3. Make your general plan long-range. Ask the question: "What do we, as God's people, need to be doing in hymnody five years from now?"

4. Make a specific one-year plan. Include the hymns you wish to use and the exact methodology to be employed in introducing, learning, and retaining them.

5. In the one-year plan chart out the expected involvement of each department of the church. Include each leader in the planning stage.

6. It is better to know five hymns well than twenty-five perfunctorily.

7. Choose hymns first on the basis of the text. Use those which are theologically rich, and avoid those which are weak, trite, or doctrinally unsound.

8. If appropriate music for a chosen text cannot be found, either find another tune setting or scrap the hymn and begin the process again. Both text and tune should be carefully scrutinized and matched.

9. Choose only hymns which are good enough to become a permanent part of the church's repertoire.

10. Ask the pastor to integrate the biblical/theological material of hymn texts in sermons and meditations, identifying by name any hymn which is used.

11. Circulate articles about the new hymns among the church's pastors, Bible teachers, small group leaders, Sunday school teachers, and choir leaders. Also, use such articles in teaching, devotions, newsletters, and bulletins when appropriate. Make posters and bulletin boards to heighten the assembly's awareness of the project. Stay away from such terms as "formal," "classic," "the good old hymns," "denominational," and "heavy."

12. To encourage the use of hymn texts as private devotional material, print them in the church paper, bulletin, or newspaper in poetic format without music.

13. Prepare the assembly, staff, and musicians for the adventure of hymn singing by acquainting them with the general approach which will be used.

14. Never let the congregation have a bad experience with a hymn. Each encounter must be successful. A totally negative bout with something new is bound to have a demoralizing effect on a congregation's future willingness to try the unfamiliar.

15. Plan to introduce a new hymn subtly, yet consistently, over a period of about eight weeks. That is, a congregation should be somewhat familiar with the tune before actually attempting to sing it for the first time. Such introductions should be indirect, not calling attention to the specific tune which is being introduced.

16. The new tune might be introduced by using it as a part of the prelude, offertory, or postlude.

17. The church orchestra could provide preludes or offertories based on the new hymn tune.

18. At some point the choir might continue the introduction of the hymn by singing a stanza as an opening acclamation, introit, call to worship, call to prayer, or benediction.

19. The hymn might also be sung as a choir anthem. It should not be "arranged" to such a degree that the assembly is not able to find and identify the tune, nor in such a way that the strength of the music is weakened by romantic, sentimental, or pop manipulation.

20. The hymn could be sung as a solo.

21. The hymn might be played as an instrumental solo for a prelude or an offertory.

22. If the hymn has a refrain (such as "For the Beauty of the Earth," *Dix*), the congregation could sing the refrain and the choir (or soloist) sing the stanzas. Staggering the amount of new material given the congregation at any one time is helpful, especially in the introductory stage.

23. After the time of introduction (between four and eight weeks) is over and the congregation is to sing the hymn for the first time, note the following things:

Keep the tempo as brisk as the particular hymn will allow.

Rehearse the accompanists ahead of time.

The accompanists should play the hymn all the way through once as the introduction.

The choir (well rehearsed in advance) should sing the tune in unison on all stanzas.

Pitch the hymn in a practical singing range.

Instruments such as trumpets might be used to reinforce the melody line.

Make it a practice to sing all stanzas. The poetic thought will be incomplete if some are left out.

Encourage the congregation to sing, but do not make a fuss over the hymn's being "new."

24. In some situations, it is possible to learn the new music in a Sunday school class, at Wednesday night service, or immediately prior to the Sunday service. Use such opportunities to good advantage.

25. After a new hymn has been learned by the congregation, use it as often as possible, especially during the first six months. Your goal is to make the hymn a normative part of the assembly's corporate worship life.

26. Subsequent repetitions of the hymn may become systematically more festive. The use of part singing, choral and instrumental descants, concertatos, modulations, reharmonizations, and certain stanzas sung a cappella will add to the celebrative nature of the new experience. Elaborateness can, however, be a detriment if the hymn is not well-established. Use discretion.

27. Let the words of the individual stanzas inspire the type of accompaniment used for each stanza.

28. Encourage various church organizations, groups, and classes to adopt a hymn as a theological/musical logo.

29. Encourage members of the congregation to use creative gifts in the composing of new hymn texts and tunes. Use them as closely graded material for specific occasions.

30. Occasionally plan an entire service as a hymn festival. Such an endeavor is a wonderful way to experience the theo-

logical, biblical, and musical richness found in our Christian heritage.

For those fortunate enough to have opportunity for intensive congregational instruction and rehearsal, the following regimen of Sir Walford Davies will be of interest. His outline is meant only to be a suggested mode of procedure, flexible and adaptable to the specific congregation and particular hymn. Note that his use of the word "verse" means stanza. His suggestions for rehearsal are as follows. Sing the:

> First line of verse 1
> First line of verse 2
> Second line of verse 2
> First two lines of verse 3
> Third line of verse 1
> Fourth line of verse 2
> The whole of verse 4

> This may appear to be fussy, but it works, because it spreads the study beyond the first verse; the repetition of the musical phrase to a fresh verbal phrase is good memory-training; and, above all, it keeps the interest alive.[14]

In all probability such a plan will not contain enough repetition for most congregations to learn particularly difficult tunes well. In that case spread the learning over two or three sessions. Once they are past the learned-note stage the real work of making the hymn a permanent part of their repertoire becomes the challenge. Hopefully, the hymn has the depth characteristic of the best of the genre, in which case several sessions could be spent in studying the text and music.[15]

Practical Matters: Range and Tempo

There are several practical considerations which will help hymn singing tremendously. The first is range. Most congregations can best manage a range from middle C to one octave above. Many tunes exceed these limits, of course. But just stand next to an average male singer attempting to sing a tune which frequently goes up to high F (fifth line, treble clef), or E, or even D. All kinds of things may happen from dropping down an octave, to singing a "harmony" note, to dropping out altogether. We can help by watching the range and using a key which mediates between the requirements of range and tessitura (the average range). One high note, for example, does not warrant putting the whole hymn down so low that the tessitura hovers around middle C, D, or E. In general, however, most hymns are too high for the average congregation and this effectively limits full participation. The following are examples of tunes which may need repitching:

> *Nicaea* ("Holy, Holy, Holy!") from E or E flat to D
>
> *Hyfrydol* ("Alleluia! Sing to Jesus," "Love Divine, All Loves Excelling," and "Come, Thou Long-Expected Jesus") from G to F
>
> *Italian Hymn* ("Come, Thou Almighty King") from G to F
>
> *Darwall* ("Rejoice, the Lord Is King!") from D to C
>
> *Landfair* ("Hail the Day That Sees Him Rise") from G to F
>
> *Cwm Rhondda* ("Guide Me, O Thou Great Jehovah") from G to F
>
> *Lobe den Herren* ("Praise to the Lord, the Almighty") from G to F.

A second consideration is tempo. Hymns are often sung too slowly. Laborious tempos are the result of a misguided understanding of musical dignity. When hymns move too slowly they lose their flow and become stilted. A good procedure is to consider the speed at which the text would be read, the mood of the text, and the style of the music. Set the tempo so that the half note value (in 4/4) moves with an easy unhurried pace in relation to the word pacing of the text, the basic unit of value (the quarter note in 4/4), and the overall sense of the text and tune together. Size and acoustics of the room, type of occasion, familiarity with the hymn, and the number of people singing will all have a bearing on the final tempo. However, a rough approximation of tempos for various hymns would be as follows:

> *Nicaea* ("Holy, Holy, Holy!"), half note = mm. 46–52
>
> *Lyons* ("O Worship the King"), quarter note = mm. 116–126
>
> *Gloria* ("Angels We Have Heard on High"), half note = mm. 54–60
>
> *Sine Nomine* ("For All the Saints"), half note = mm. 53–58

Aurelia ("The Church's One Foundation"), half note = mm. 48–54.

The Hymnal 1982 includes in the accompaniment edition tempo suggestions for each hymn.[16] Another help is William J. Reynolds' *Congregational Singing*.[17] These resources can be useful to the music minister who is leading a drive to encourage the assembly in hymn singing and needs assistance in choosing tempi.

Unfamiliar Types of Hymns

Within the context of this present study in which music is seen as a discipling agent, it is important to note that unfamiliar hymn categories which are more plain and austere than those familiar to the congregation, should be introduced at an appropriate time. According to Alice Parker, six common hymn categories are: chants and processionals, psalter hymns, chorales, classic hymns, folk hymns, and spirituals.[18] From this list, hymns based on chant have special value for helping congregations move from the contemporary bent for the pleasurable to a more mature embracing of the disciplined. If congregations are prepared for the experience, chant hymns such as "Come, Holy Ghost, Our Souls Inspire"[19] or "Creator of the Stars of Night"[20] can be helpful. If classic hymns are the norm ("Come, Thou Almighty King"[21]), then perhaps the chorale type or the folk type might be the next step. If all types of hymns are well represented in the assembly's hymn singing, then we might concentrate on expanding their repertoire, emphasizing those which are less familiar and have a more excellent textual and musical value. Simultaneously we might drop others that are not the best examples of a particular genre.

Gospel Songs

Some churches have a long tradition of gospel song usage to the exclusion of, and to the detriment of, the church's normal hymnody. Though there has been a continuing dispute between the advocates of the two genres, by and large the issue is not nearly so divisive as it has been in the past.[22] There are now people who have never thought about the differences between gospel songs and hymns, assuming them to be identical categories. Indeed, the Hymn Society of America has attempted to get

away from an overly rigid definition of the term "hymn"; by
suggesting that a hymn be defined simply as "a congregational
song."[23] But in order to evaluate the quality of hymnody important to a discipling music ministry, we need to differentiate
between the two. It is well that the bitterness between the two
camps has dissipated. But there was a reason for this historic
rivalry, and the reasons are still valid. The gospel song tends
toward the subjective and the individualistic. It is "me" and
"self" oriented. The subject matter is limited. Testimonies of
personal salvation (or some variation thereof) are its main theme,
but others are noteworthy: heaven, one's blessings as a Christian,
and personal aspirations for living the Christian life. The music
is usually simplistic, even trite, and the literary quality of the
poetry is generally poor. There is usually little theological scope
or depth. Historically, the gospel song is a primitive (perhaps
naive) musical form which mirrored the developing subjectivistic
tendencies of the nineteenth and early twentieth centuries. All
told, the gospel song is not the form which we wish to promote
if we are after great spiritual maturity.

Our plea here is to consider carefully the relative merits
of gospel songs and hymns. Surely one would not put James
Rowe's "Love Lifted Me" (example 31) on the same level as
Charles Wesley's "Love Divine, All Loves Excelling" (example
32). Compare the two.

The text of "Love Lifted Me" is not wrong (though
some of its imagery may be questionable), but it is not profound,
comprehensive, or biblically connected. Centered around "me,"
it is simply immature. In a discipling music ministry, hymnody
needs maturity. Let us be clear, however, in stating that congregations who are at the level of "Love Lifted Me" should use it.
But if maturity is our goal, we should move on as soon as possible
to a more penetrating, developed, and informed hymnody.

Chorus Singing

The former issue of gospel songs vs. hymns has been
replaced by the current controversy between choruses vs. hymns.
Many congregations, pastors, and musicians believe that hymn
texts actually get in the way of worship! They believe hymns have
too many words, too many ideas, and too many theological
categories. Self-gratification is minimal in hymns. In our subjec-

tivistic culture rationality and mind are thought to be a hindrance to "real" worship (believed to be a matter of feeling). Choruses "work better."

Historically, it may be that the most enduring legacy of the gospel song is the use of refrains or choruses apart from the stanzas (the gospel song uses a stanza/refrain form). As gospel songs came to play an increasingly important part in the evangelical church's liturgy in the early decades of the twentieth century, refrains began to take on a musical life of their own. Their popularity eventually led to a separate chorus genre with new ones being composed without stanzas at all.

Any need for careful intellectual involvement or thought is pretty much eliminated when only refrains are used. By their very nature choruses are not profound in text or music. The focus is on the generation of religious emotion. Having been emancipated from holding a hymnal, congregations are free to close their eyes, clap their hands, or lift their hands in praise and adoration.

The renewal movement and charismatic revival have further popularized the singing of choruses and refrains. Presuming themselves estranged from emotional involvement in worship, those who sang choruses regarded them as a symbol of their newfound freedom and fervor. Singing these easily memorizable one-idea songs (often a verse or less of scripture) was thought to generate or maintain religious experience. Hymn singing came to be seen as the "old way" and looked upon as unimportant if not impotent. Whether by design or not, certain churches have opted to embrace exclusively (except for a token "grand old" hymn now and again) what has come to be known as the worship and praise chorus. This practice is strengthened by organizations within established churches, such as the Roman Catholic and Episcopal Cursillo movements and various other renewal ministries which tend to use mainly chorus-type songs in their gatherings. Religious fervor is usually high in these meetings, and chorus singing has come to be identified with such zeal. Invariably there comes pressure to include more and more such material during the regular services of worship. Hymns are seen as cold and formal, and therefore less "spiritual"; choruses are believed to be warmer and informal, and obviously more "spiritual."

In any case, the gospel song and chorus movement in their extreme forms are but musical examples of the lack of discipline in our society. The centuries-long move toward more preoccupation with self has shown up in the denuding and emasculating of much content from the church's song. Christians have taken the easy way. The extreme humanistic self-pleasuring which has popularized chorus singing has removed worthy genres of song from worship. We use choruses simply because we like them better than anything else. That is the criterion of use. They require little of us. We have become used to their Pavlovian inducement of religious emotion; we like the inactivity of the intellect and the beat which is often accompanied by clapping and dancing or some other physical manifestation. We are used to the repetitiveness of words and music that mesmerize the singer into accepting religious platitudes and clichés.

Interestingly, many churches who have come to utilize choruses almost exclusively often believe they are returning to the worship practices of the New Testament church. They often refer to a symbiotic relationship between "deep" worship and the use of choruses. There is no doubt that those pastors, music directors, and people who have begun to sing this type of music do so because, in addition to being easy and pleasurable, they believe them to be more spiritual. Our contention here is that in actuality the opposite is true. Exclusive use of choruses tends to produce a people who have the same depth of spirituality as the music they sing. The result is a faith which lacks depth, is simplistic, pleasure-oriented, emotionalistic, intellectually weak, undisciplined, and prone to the changeability of feelings. The end result of nothing but chorus singing is immaturity.

Our cultural shift toward image (television, video, and cinema) has caused some churches to use the overhead projector as a kind of chorus prompter. Large screens display religious scenes in a kind of multi-media worship event. Words and occasionally music are also projected on the screen for teaching new choruses or for newcomers who have not as yet memorized the old ones. But does this aversion to reading do a disservice to the making of mature Christians? If we take away the necessity of reading from the hymnal in worship, perhaps it will not be long before the Bible will be next! The belief that reading something from a book makes it less valuable in worship is a cultural phenomenon which the church must resist. It is in fact primarily through the written Word that God communicates to us. Let us not discount the importance of print. The regular and systematic use of the hymnal can help normalize the use of the printed page in our "post-Gutenberg" age. Choruses tend not to support this bias toward print because they are easily memorized. And even if our entire body of hymnody were memorizable, reinforcing with the eye the material one already has committed to memory just strengthens it that much more.

It is unfortunate that pastors and church musicians have so readily capitulated to the swing from hymnody to choruses. Perhaps it is unfair to lay too much blame for this trend at their feet. Having the pragmatic bent useful in working with people, pastors and musicians have been caught up in a direction much more sweeping and more related to our general culture than they have realized. They have known that something seemed to work and have not looked beyond that fact. Choruses have become popular not only because they mirror certain philosophical aspects of culture, but because of the aggressive marketing of many music publishers and producers. Chorus books, recordings, and tapes, as well as the instruction and example of many worship leaders have greatly influenced the religious public toward chorus singing. The church has been unwittingly caught up in a philosophical and economic push it found irresistible.

It would be incorrect to leave the impression that chorus singing should be avoided altogether. Not so. There are values in non-exclusive use of chorus singing. Some of these are inherent in the genre: their simplicity, memorability, and their directness in addressing God. Without a book to read and hold, worshipers can close their eyes, shutting out distractions, and can raise their hands in adoration and surrender. This often proves helpful to worshipers. Choruses are able to open up the emotional life of the believer, helping one develop a warm and heartfelt worship. On balance, however, it is the church's hymnody that must be fostered above that of chorus singing. As a substitute for hymnody, it fails since choruses have a limited ability to disciple the assembly because of their lack of depth.

Hymnody as a Discipline

If our congregations are to be mature, disciplined, and knowledgeable men and women who are all that God intends them to be, we must revive hymnody with wholehearted enthusiasm. The biblical predilection for forms which are content-oriented cannot be ignored. A token effort will not suffice. Music directors, pastors, and congregations must be convinced deep in their souls that hymns are important. They must have the unshakable conviction that hymn singing is God's will for his church. A rationalization which puts it on a purely elective basis leads to failure.

This commitment must be shared by all members of the church staff. Hymns are so interconnected with preaching, teaching, prayer, worship, and witness that leaders must assume them normative within their specific areas of responsibility. That is to say that hymn singing must be churchwide, in Sunday school, prayer meetings, youth rallies, private devotions, and family prayers. To isolate hymn singing in a rigid Sunday morning worship "box" is to bury it. Careful and comprehensive planning is necessary. Everyone in the body should become involved.

Many things contribute to the demise of parish hymn singing: unfamiliarity, seemingly irrelevant texts, difficulty of imagery, poor acoustics (too short a reverberation time), inadequate pianos and organs or pianists and organists, the expense of purchasing hymnals, the effort needed to sing hymns, the time of the service (too early or too late for good singing), the range of the tunes, or the lack of a "beat." For many of our children and youth who have been brought up on choruses, hymn singing has never been a normal part of worship. Worship leaders brave enough to include it often meet with great resistance. Many are tempted to succumb to popular opinion and simply include a steady diet of chorus singing. This will effect a positive response and fulfill the need for feeling that the congregational singing was a "success." Perhaps it is true that we are now in a "post-hymnal" era.[24] If this is so in any given church, a discipling music ministry must resurrect the hymnal and reintroduce it to the assembly.

Many Christians complain that they do not understand hymns. This is to be expected, since the very best hymns have poetry which is thoughtfully and intricately crafted. Such artistry may cause people to think that the poetry is too obscure; words or word pictures are no longer relevant; the language is too difficult to understand; or there are too many concepts to grasp. Or perhaps hymns are simply considered boring, out of style, or just "not my thing." Whether these charges are true or not, the point here is that hymn singing is an established scriptural norm for the church. Disciples do not base their actions on what they prefer but on biblical precepts. Discipleship takes effort. Hymn singing which is edifying to the body requires more than merely dusting off the songbooks on Sunday morning, turning to a "token" hymn because we think we should, and "using" that hymn as a steppingstone to the "real" music ministry of chorus singing. Hymn singing requires the work of the pastor, the musicians, and above all, the congregation.

There is a price to pay if hymn singing is to have its rightful place within the worship of the redeemed. If the poetry is obscure, the language too difficult, or imagery irrelevant, teaching needs to set right our deficiencies. There is nothing sacrosanct about intellectual poverty. We are made in God's image with the capacity to learn. To dismiss a whole biblical genre of song simply because we believe some of it to be too difficult is almost as bad as dismissing it simply because it isn't liked, or doesn't "work." Part of the music director's ministry is to help the congregation utilize our hymnic heritage with competency and evangelistic zeal. If we simply relegate hymns to the ash heap we are wiping out in one stroke a body of material (some of which has been sung since before the time of our Lord) which is one of the most important musical ways, if not the most important way, to Christian maturity. Without hymn singing we play right into the hands of those who would remove content from Christianity and reduce it to subjective feeling. Removing hymn singing from worship is but another means of trivializing our faith—a dangerous, unbiblical practice.

Increasing the depth of the assembly's repertoire of hymns will yield rewards in the maturing of the assembly. Hymns which are fastidiously sound theologically and correspondingly worthy musically are the only congregational musical genre we have for expressing the incredible richness of our Christian faith. Without them the church would be much poorer, the body more feeble, and each member's spiritual growth needlessly stunted. Music directors need to begin (or continue, as the case may be) the task of implementing a hymnological revival for the theological and musical edification of our people. We must practice now for the ages to come.

Spiritual Songs

After psalms and hymns, spiritual songs represent the third category of Christian song mentioned by St. Paul in Ephesians 5:19 and Colossians 3:16. There have been various interpretations of the term. Some have treated psalms, hymns, and spiritual songs as synonyms. Others have believed spiritual songs to be a distinct type of song, such as the improvised ecstatic songs practiced by many eastern religions, or perhaps the extended melismas of certain types of chant such as that found in the jubilus of a Gregorian alleluia. Still others have believed spiritual songs to mean simply singing spiritually or with the anointing of the Holy Spirit on the singer and the song. Occasionally spiritual songs have been equated with the gospel song and/or choruses.

It is generally agreed that spiritual songs have an immediacy and improvisatory quality which distinguishes them from the psalm and the hymn. The adjective *pneumatikos* (spiritual) which describes song or ode in Ephesians 5:19 and Colossians 3:16 is the same adjective used by St. Paul in 1 Corinthians 12:1 and 14:1 to describe "spiritual" gifts, specifically those which are supernatural and hence do not depend upon the rationality of humans but upon special inspiration from God. The operative thing in spiritual songs is the Holy Spirit who comes to influence the singer and the song in much the same way that he directs the believer in the operation of spiritual gifts. Spiritual songs are songs prompted by the Holy Spirit, and they are most often sung in an unknown language.

The present phenomenon of singing in the Spirit (impromptu singing in an unknown tongue) and, in a limited way, praise singing (impromptu singing in the vernacular), are examples of modern day spiritual songs. Such practice has as its main component a heartfelt love for God of immeasurable magnitude. Under the inspiration of the Spirit individuals express their praise by singing in a tongue or uttering such phrases in the vernacular as: "Thank you, Jesus," "Praise you, Lord," "Hallelujah," "I love you, Father," "Praise the name of Jesus." These variously improvised utterances, though sung together simultaneously, are sung with varying tempos, rhythms, and pitches according to the inclination of each individual worshiper. Individual spontaneity is one of the distinguishing marks of singing in the spirit.

Such expressions have four general musical character-istics. First, most of the utterance is sung on one pitch in the manner we have previously described as cantillation or mono-tonic recitation. The rhythm is that of speech and the overall effect not unlike that of chant. Second, melismas (more than one note to a syllable) are often employed. Any single syllable of any word may be used for the singing of many notes in one long continuous string. There is complete freedom to sing the Spirit-prompted utterances in an improvisatory manner. Third, nor-mally only one chord (the tonic) forms the harmonic basis of the spiritual song. This congregational improvisation is such that at any given time there will appear in the musical texture the simultaneous singing of the root, third, and fifth of this solitary chord, each individual choosing whatever notes he or she wishes. In addition, passing tones, neighbor notes, and other embellish-ments are included. Usually most of the words will be declaimed as we have stated, on a single pitch, be it the root, third, or fifth. Nonharmonic tones will be employed less frequently and are most often reserved for melismas. Fourth, there are no set beginnings or endings such as the intonation and final cadence common to the Gregorian psalm tones.

When everyone worships simultaneously in this extem-poraneous fashion, each person singing individually without re-gard for coordinating with another's song, the whole effect is similar to the gentle strumming of a harp. The diatonic notes of the C major scale, for example, will all be represented at any given time with the notes of the tonic chord predominant. Singing in this fashion is best done a cappella, an important consideration for directors to note. Instrumental music intrudes on such expression: first, by mechanically manipulating the song's execution (such as holding down a single chord on the organ ad infinitum to instigate and maintain the singing of the congre-gation's "improvised" praises); second, by causing confusion through any changes of harmony, which, of course, will not agree with the single chordal structure of the improvised spiri-tual song.

The singing of so many different expressions concur-rently might seem at first to be confusing. But this isn't the case because individual praises to God are melded together as the corporate body lifts its unknown song in adoration to the King of kings. For musicians it is but another example of musical and textual counterpoint. Worshipers who are carefully taught find it a way of expressing to God their most personal praise within a corporate musical structure. Such extemporaneous worship can be extremely meaningful. When done decently and in order, it is another way the music ministry disciples the congregation toward spiritual maturity.

Reevaluating Recent Musical Trends

Romanticism Revisited

We have already dealt with romanticism. But perhaps a further statement in our present context would be appropriate. Romanticism is more than a historical period, a convenient term used by music historians and music theorists. It is a continuing phenomenon. A perusal of what is presently being written and consumed shows that most church music is essentially romantic in one way or another. There are notable exceptions of course, but on the average, churchgoers still prefer expressiveness through compositional emotionalism, intemperance, and manipulation than expressiveness through compositional rationality, restraint, and objectivity.

Romanticism does much harm to the maturing processes of church music. The feeling we get through this music becomes the focus of the composition. Brought about by our self-concerned culture, worshipers immerse themselves in the experiential and the affective, believing that church music has failed unless melodramatic hype is present to stimulate and arouse. As an emotionalistic device, it engenders ever higher states of emotional satisfaction in the believer. Rather than allow feeling to be a result, we have made it music's chief purpose; rather than a reaction it has been re-formed into an action; rather than a consequent it has become an antecedent. The centrality of musical emotionalism has become so pervasive that we seldom challenge its domination.

An example of contemporary preference for romantic expression is the popular Albert Hay Malotte setting of the Lord's Prayer. Matthew 6 begins with Jesus' admonishing his disciples not to "make a spectacle" of their faith. Let there be no "personal flaunting" to herald personal piety, no exhibitionism.

One should be secretive and modest in prayer. But Malotte, a California theater organist active in writing movie background scores and for a time director of music for the Walt Disney Studios, sets this prayer to music that can only be described as most immodest.

A brief look at the music shows it to be highly romantic. Taken together, the harmony, melody, and rhythm give a musical impression often termed "tear-jerking." And of course that is what it is designed to do. The triplet-figure accompaniment, the rising melodic line, the chromaticism, the harmonic turns, the dynamic extremes, and the pretentiousness of the climax give the piece a flamboyance and show quite in keeping with the subjectivity and romanticism ingrained in the consciousness of most assemblies. The piece produces great gushing feelings, maudlin sentiment, and sensual ecstasy, masterfully evoking self-indulgent sensation.

However, the romanticism of the Malotte composition is quite out of step with Jesus' instructions and intentions. The piece is showy. It "stands on the street corner" and draws attention to itself. There is little of the simplicity, grace, and straightforwardness implicit in the text of the prayer and explicit in Christ's directives:

> And when you pray, you must not be like the hypocrites; for they love to stand and pray in the synagogues and at the street corners, that they may be seen by men. Truly, I say to you, they have received their reward. But when you pray, go into your room and shut the door and pray to your Father who is in secret; and your Father who sees in secret will reward you.[25]

Do we get the same thrill when the prayer is spoken as we do from listening to the Malotte rendition? Obviously not. The music is the key factor here. It produces the emotion. The text is just peripheral. Without this particular musical setting the Lord's prayer becomes much less romantic and appealing. The emotionalism is gone.

Example 33, however, is more simple, straightforward, and direct. There is no attempt to put "emotion" into the music. It is a setting whose aim is to simply be a vehicle for praying the prayer. The music breathes the spirit in which the prayer was given. Its asceticism is its strength. The objectivity of the music allows that great emotion when singing the prayer be the result of praying the text—not a result of the romantic manipulation of the music. In a word, this setting has discipline.

Ultraromanticism in church music works against our aim of maturing people in God, producing musical emotion which is believed by congregations to be genuinely religious. Romanticism is able to counterfeit the heart-felt response we want in people when confronted by the truth of the Almighty. Romantically engendered emotion is a human centered response to musical stimuli.

The confusion between true spiritual emotion and musically engendered emotion often results in people taking an uninformed position on the subject. On the one hand we may encourage romantic manipulation in the mistaken belief that it is authentic religious emotion. Ironically, this only makes the congregation spiritually immature because it focuses on the emotion itself. On the other hand there is a danger that all emotion will be mistrusted and steps will be taken to make faith unemotional. One great part of our being is then treated as alien to faith, stereotyping faith as cold, calculating, and propositional. This is also a dead end. If the assembly discards extreme romantic worship forms, music may more directly address its goal. Disciplined vehicles of integrity, free of the need for manipulating emotion, can stress a leaner music which no longer is concerned with self and its feelings, but instead focuses on God and his praise. At that point genuine religious emotion can be expected to fire the soul with passion and zeal for our Lord.

Dynamics and Sound Amplification

We do not have precise information of the dynamic level of music prior to the Renaissance and not much more immediately afterward. But it is generally conceded by scholars that the music of the Middle Ages was modest and not excessive, neither too soft nor too loud. Since self-expression by the composer and performer was not music's prime purpose as in Romanticism, techniques which were later regarded as expressive were of little concern. During the development of humanism and through the Age of Reason and the Enlightenment to the present day, personal expression of feelings has become more and more important. Increasing dynamic levels became one means through which expressiveness was achieved. It must be remembered that this increasing need paralleled the rise of people's self-orienta-tion and sense of their own importance. With the advent of electrical amplification, musicians dramatically bolstered their potential for self-expression and self-aggrandizement. Some mu-sic's dynamic level has even reached the threshold of pain. In fact, hearing loss among rock stars is not uncommon. As the need for human autonomy continued, the microphone and am-plifier's excessive sound levels became tools for demonstrating the musician's control over reality.

The popular music of our day, the true nerve center of contemporary musical life, has become louder and louder. It is almost as if rock musicians have sought to beat the world into submission by virtue of their musical dominance over the envi-ronment. And the louder the music, the more raw and primitive the sound becomes. As sound levels rise, a proportionate lack of sensitivity is engendered in the listener. An aesthetic hardness and callousness sets in.

Much contemporary Christian music emulates the same searing decibel levels as its secular rock counterpart. The results are the same: (1) the self-conferred license for attempting to achieve personal power over the world promotes anarchistic sounds and sound levels; and (2) religious pop musicians con-clude they are emancipated from the need for discipline and restraint.

Church musicians can help the maturity of believers by limiting sound amplification. Allowing music to speak naturally and freely, without electrical mechanisms multiplying the decibel level, will be a new experience for many worshipers. It will be discovered that unamplified sound has an honesty and simplicity which matches well the unadorned plainness of the gospel. Am-plifying sound in an extremely large auditorium commensurate with the natural output of the choir or soloist is not the issue. But to make the sound "bigger" and "better" than it actually is, or to make a statement by screaming, making the music ear-piercing for the kick it gives, must be regarded as ill-advised, even illogical, for in heightening sound output above that which musicians are naturally capable of, artistic expression is left far behind. Oppression takes its place. Through extreme loudness and decibel overkill, an insistent, thumping, hammering, coer-cive impression is driven into the listener's consciousness until he or she becomes so numb that the sensory system shuts down.

The self has not been expressed as much as it has been tyranni-
cally impressed on the hearer. Musically, a demand is made that
listeners, against their own wills, participate in the artistic vision
of the performing group. The primary purpose of excessively
loud music is to make the self so powerful that listeners are
forced to accede to the artist's statement. Such music is manipulative, coercive, and mind-deadening to say the least. A more
disciplined approach is needed, one in which expressiveness
results from honesty, forthrightness, and clarity of presentation.
Musical coercion is anathema.

The Pipe Organ

The pipe organ (and its electronic equivalent) has been
the single most important instrument in the Western church
(other than the human voice). There are several reasons for this:
it has (1) the carrying power necessary to accompany large
numbers of people; (2) many tonal colors which give variety to
the ensemble; (3) versatility, needing only one person to play it.

But the most important reason why the classic organ is
the church instrument par excellance is that it is the most objective instrument we have. It is not as subject to excess romanticism as other instruments. The organ, in other words, does not
lend itself well to emotionalism. This is one reason why organ
repertoire was so limited in the Romantic Era. Its mechanism
prohibits the performer from executing satisfactorily the techniques which give music the emotionalistic pull required of the
genre. But the inability to portray sentimentality is the precise
trait which makes it a good church instrument, since theistic
doctrine, values, and standards are not fanciful flights of idealized notions of sentimentalized feelings, changing with every
whim of human frailty. No. Church dogma is based on un-
changeable reality. Objective in its truth, it is not subject to
individualistic caprice. Musically, the organ represents such objectivity well. Its straightforwardness makes it suitable for musically supporting belief which is more like the rock of Gibraltar
than the changeability of the weather. Our faith is founded not
on emotionalism but on the immutability of God, and the organ
comes the closest of any instrument in describing that objective
quality. Its support of a liturgy based on God rather than on
humanity is unsurpassed.

It may well be that worship will be further influenced in the years to come by the humanistic tendencies of emotionalism and sentimentality. If so, the pipe organ can help counter such influences. That it does not lend itself to the theatrics of manipulation will help keep the music on a more objective plane. Of course theatre organs and certain electronic organs with wide vibratos, romanticized sounds, and synthesized percussion divisions are not what we are referring to. This type of instrument is fine for skating rinks or for soap operas. But it is not a true musical representation of our faith. On the other hand, the classic pipe organ can help the discipling role of ministry tremendously by its musical objectivity.

The Importance of Good Acoustics

Good acoustics are the single most important physical property necessary to successful music making—congregational, choral, instrumental, or solo. Yet we find many church buildings with very poor acoustics. Dry and dead with hardly any reverberation time, musical sounds without a proper acoustical environment are a detriment to music: singing is poor, participation suffers, musical vitality is eradicated, tone becomes brittle and harsh, and musical projection is inhibited. Such characteristics result from designing buildings for intimacy and comfort: (1) carpeted aisles, chancels, and choir areas; (2) low ceilings (often constructed with acoustical tile or other sound deadening material); (3) noisy air conditioning and heating systems; (4) general materials which may look nice but absorb sound rather than reflect it; and (5) a too small ratio of enclosed space to the seating area. Amplification systems cannot compensate for or correct acoustical problems caused by such design flaws.

A room with three seconds of reverberation when filled to its maximum seating capacity is an optimum compromise between speech and music. (This time span was arrived at by a joint council of the American Institute of Architects, the American Guild of Organists and the Associated Pipe Organ Builders of America.[26]) Such a room should have a sound "decay" which allows for a large initial reverberation drop in the first one and one half seconds and a more gradual one over the remaining one and one half seconds. Such a decay curve will generally give tone its needed harmonic development and will tend to disperse the sound evenly throughout the room. A general comparison would be to that of a tiled shower stall. Music comes alive with such acoustics! We must note that for churches which emphasize congregational participation in such things as testimonies, prayers, the exercise of spiritual gifts, or personal exhortations from the nave, a good reverberation time will result in word intelligibility throughout the room from any point in the room without amplification (except in the very largest of buildings).

Taped Accompaniments

Another subject for discipling music ministries to consider is the use of taped accompaniments. They should be avoided. Though they have been used for many decades for practice situations (such as that for concerto soloists or for vocalists who wished to practice with an orchestra before the performance), they have only recently been in vogue in churches. Such devices are really alien to the whole idea of artistic and spiritual inspiration in performance. Their use is much more detrimental than helpful.

The essence of any musical performance is spontaneity. In addition, church music needs to be free to respond to the promptings of the Spirit: a new tempo, an emphasis on this or that phrase or word, holding such and such a note a bit longer than usual, or singing with slightly different mood and pacing. Little of this is possible when taped accompaniments are used. The canned approach demands a sameness which makes every performance clone-like. Soloists must meet the predetermined and unchanging demands of the tape. Hence, performers become automatons.

The reasons why taped accompaniments are so appealing are obvious. People who listen to religious music over the radio, stereo, or CD player get used to the sounds of a full orchestra or band. When just the organ or piano is used, these accompaniments seem unexciting and bland by comparison. Also, tapes have a mechanically polished expertise which live accompaniments seldom match.

However, the artistic and spiritual sacrifice is too great a price to pay. This is especially true when we consider the necessity of church music to be pliable under the Spirit's guidance. Very little can be done to alter musical interpretation when the tape just keeps rolling along. It would be better to use piano, organ or other instruments, or even sing a cappella than to treat church music in such a manner. When tapes are used we are essentially listening to a recording. The spontaneity is gone.

Music directors will find that eliminating taped accompaniments will be a discipline with many benefits: (1) congregations will have to lower their musical entertainment expectations and concentrate on the spareness of essentials; (2) performers will need commitment to practice with real people instead of a tape—not as easy or as convenient; (3) performers will also need to relearn the art of live performance and begin to cultivate a sensitivity to the Spirit's influence on their performance practice; and (4) the musical gifts of the body will be developed as those who are able to play instruments will find their talent needed and welcomed. Above all, an embracing of live music over recorded music will serve to give notice to the corporate assembly that honesty in doing what we have been gifted with and accepting the limits of our gifts, not attempting to be more "professional" than we are, will give a wholesomeness and healthiness to our music making that is as refreshing as it is good for us. Discipling music ministry in this way makes us that much more mature.

Example 22
Psalm 13:1–6
From *Gradual Psalms: Year B*, compiled by Richard Crocker, © Church
Pension Fund, 1980. Used by permission.

REFRAIN

Give light to my eyes, O   Lord.

PSALM 13   TONE VI

1 *How long*, O LORD?
    will you forget me / for év-er?*
      how long will you / hide your fáce from me?
2 How long shall I have perplexity in my mind,
    and grief in my heart, day / af-tér day?*
      how long shall my enemy / tri-umph ó-ver me?

                                     REFRAIN

3 *Look up* – on me and answer me, / O LÓRD my God;*
    give light to my eyes, / lest Ī sleép in death;
4 Lest my enemy say, "I have pre - / vailed ó-ver him,"*
    and my foes rejoice that / I häve fáll-en.

                                     REFRAIN

5 *But Ī* put my trust in / your mér-cy;*
    my heart is joyful because / of your sáv-ing help.
6 I will sing to the LORD, for he has dealt with / me
                    rích-ly;*
    I will praise the Name / of the LÓRD Most High.

                                     REFRAIN

Example 23
Psalm 13:1–6
Transcription.
From Richard Crocker, *Gradual Psalms: Year B*, © Church Hymnal
Corporation, 1980. Used by permission.

Example 24
Psalm 24:1–6
Copy of actual page reproduced by permission from The Hymnary Press
and James E. Barrett.

PSALM 24:1-6

Lift up your heads, O gates; and the King of glo—ry shall come in.

The earth is the Lord's and /all that is in it, *
    the world and /all who dwell therein.
For it is he who founded /it upon the seas*
    and made it firm upon the /rivers of the deep. [ANTIPHON]

"Who can ascend the /hill of the Lord? *
    and who can stand /in his holy place?"
"Those who have clean /hands and a pure heart,*
    who have not pledged themselves to falsehood,
    nor sworn by /what is a fraud. [ANTIPHON]

They shall receive a /blessing from the Lord*
    and a just reward from the God of /their salvation."
Such is the generation of /those who seek him,
    of those who seek your face, O /God of Jacob. [ANTIPHON]

Tone VII.8

Copyright 1982 by James E. Barrett in The Psalmnary.
Permission for reproduction in service bulletin granted by The Hymnary Press.

Lift up your heads, O gates; and the King of glo—ry shall come in.

Copyright 1982 by James E. Barrett.

4 Advent A

E G A C D
CM6-9 Am7-11

Example 25
Psalm 24:1–6   The Psalmnary James E. Barrett
Transcription.
Copy of actual page reproduced by permission from The Hymnary Press
and James E. Barrett.

Psalm 24:1-6

Antiphon
Lift up your heads, O gates; and the King of glo-ry shall come in.

The earth is the LORD'S and all that is in it, * the world and all

who dwell there-in.

For it is he who founded it up-on the seas* and made it firm upon the

riv-ers of the deep.
Antiphon

"Who can ascend the hill of the Lord? * and who can stand in his ho-ly place?"

"Those who have clean hands and a pure heart,*

who have not pledged themselves to falsehood, nor sworn by what is a fraud.
Antiphon

They shall receive a bless-ing from the Lord *

and a just reward from the God of their sal-va-tion."

Such is the generation of those who seek Him,*

of those who seek your face, O God of Ja-cob.
Antiphon

Example 26
Simplified Anglican chant
Music copyright © 1979, Robert Knox Kennedy. Used by permission.

1979, Robert Knox Kennedy.

1   The LORD is my / shepherd; *
        I shall not be in / want.

2   He makes me lie down in green / pastures *
        and leads me beside still / waters.

3   He revives my / soul *
        and guides me along right pathways for his Name's / sake.

4   Though I walk through the valley of the shadow of death,
        I shall fear no / evil; *
            for you are with me;
            your rod and your staff, they / comfort me.

5   You spread a table before me in the presence of those
                        who / trouble me; *
            you have anointed my head with oil,
            and my cup is running / over.

6   Surely your goodness and mercy shall follow me all the days
                        of my / life *
            and I will dwell in the house of the LORD for / ever.

Example 27
Psalm 23
Transcription.
Chant, Psalm 23, music copyright © 1979, Robert Knox Kennedy. Used
by permission.

Robert Knox Kennedy

1 The Lord is my shep-herd;* I shall not be in want.

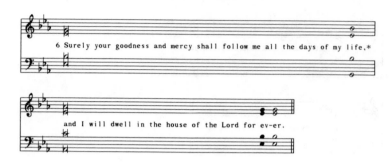

6 Surely your goodness and mercy shall follow me all the days of my life,*

and I will dwell in the house of the Lord for ev-er.

Example 28
Single Anglican chant here, Psalm 100
From *The Anglican Chant Psalter*, © 1987, edited by Alex Wyton, published by the Church Hymnal Corporation.

John Stainer

1 Be joyful in the LORD, 'all you 'lands; *
   serve the LORD with gladness
   and come before his 'presence 'with a 'song.

2 Know this: The LORD him'self is 'God; *
   he himself has made us, and we are his;
   we are his 'people and the 'sheep of his 'pasture.

3 Enter his gates with thanksgiving;
   go into his 'courts with 'praise; *
   give thanks to him and 'call up'on his 'Name.

4 For the LORD is good;
   his mercy is 'ever'lasting; *
   and his faithfulness en'dures from 'age to 'age.

Example 29
Psalm 100
Transcription.
From *The Anglican Chant Psalter*, © 1987, edited by Alex Wyton, published by the Church Hymnal Corporation.

Psalm 100

John Stainer

1 Be joyful in the LORD, all you lands;* serve the LORD with gladness

and come before his pres-ence with a song. 2 Know this: The LORD him-self

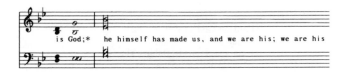

is God;* he himself has made us, and we are his; we are his

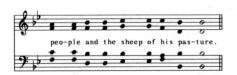

peo-ple and the sheep of his pas-ture.

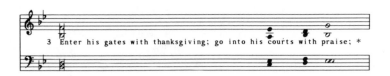

3 Enter his gates with thanksgiving; go into his courts with praise; *

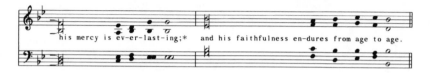

Example 30
Psalm 8
Metrical Psalm
© *A New Metrical Psalter*, by Christopher L. Webber. Used with permission.
May be sung to the tune *Azmon*, O For a Thousand Tongues to Sing.

C.M.

1. O Lord our God, in all the world
        Your glory we acclaim;
    The mouths of infants, children's lips,
        Your majesty proclaim.

2. You set against the enemy
        A fortress high and strong
    To quell the adversary's might
        And those who do us wrong.

3. When I look up and see the moon
        And stars in heaven above,
    Lord, why should you remember us
        And visit us in love?

4. Yet you have made us only less
        Than angels, and you crown
    Our lives with glory, give us rule
        To earth's remotest bound.

5. All sheep and oxen, beasts and birds,
        We rule in your great Name;
    O Lord our God, in all the world
        Your glory we acclaim.

Example 31
Love Lifted Me

1. I was sink-ing deep in sin, Far from the peace-ful shore, Ver-y deep-ly
2. All my heart to Him I give, Ev-er to Him I'll cling, In His bless-ed
3. Souls in dan-ger, look a-bove, Je-sus com-plete-ly saves; He will lift you

stained with-in, Sink-ing to rise no more; But the Mas-ter of the sea
pres-ence live, Ev-er His prais-es sing; Love so might-y and so true
by His love Out of the an-gry waves; He's the Mas-ter of the sea,

Heard my de-spair-ing cry, From the wa-ters lift-ed me, Now safe am I.
Mer-its my soul's best songs; Faith-ful, lov-ing ser-vice, too, To Him be-longs.
Bil-lows His will o-bey; He your Sav-ior wants to be, Be saved to-day.

Refrain

Love lift-ed me! Love lift-ed me! When noth-ing
e-ven me! e-ven me!

1. else could help, Love lift-ed me.
2. Love lift-ed me.

TEXT: James Rowe
MUSIC: Howard E. Smith

SAFETY
7.6.7.6.7.6.7.4. with Refrain

Example 32
Love Divine, All Loves Excelling
From *The Hymnal 1982*, © Church Pension Fund. Used by permission.

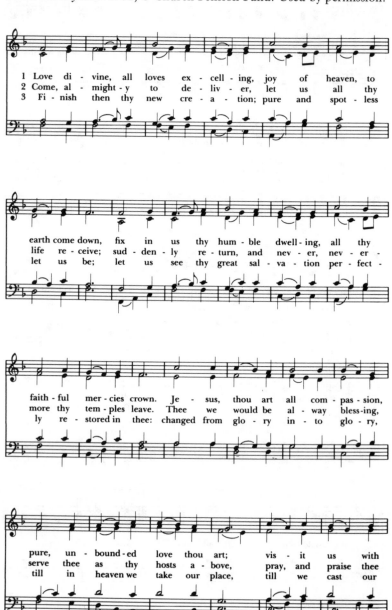

thy   sal - va - tion,   en - ter   ev - ery   trem-bling heart.
with - out   ceas - ing,   glo - ry   in   thy   per - fect   love.
crowns be - fore   thee,   lost   in   won - der,   love, and   praise.

Words: Charles Wesley (1707-1788)
Music: *Hyfrydol*, Rowland Hugh Prichard (1811-1887)

87. 87. D

Example 33
The Lord's Prayer
From *The Hymnal 1982*, © Church Pension Fund. Used by permission.

Our   Fa - ther, who   art   in   hea - ven,   hal - low - ed

be   thy   Name,   thy   king - dom come,   thy   will   be   done,

on   earth   as   it   is   in   hea - ven.   Give   us   this   day   our

dai - ly   bread.   And   for - give   us   our   tres - pas - ses,

as   we   for - give those who   tres - pass   a - gainst   us.   And   lead

us   not   in - to   temp - ta - tion,   but   de - liv - er   us

from   e - vil.   For   thine   is   the   king - dom,   and   the power,

and   the   glo - ry,   for   ev - er   and   ev - er.   A - men.

Setting: Plainsong; adapt. Charles Winfred Douglas (1867-1944)

Notes

1. Richard Crocker, *Gradual Psalms: Year A, Gradual Psalms: Year B, Gradual Psalms: Year C* (New York: The Church Hymnal Corporation, 1980).

2. James Litton, *The Plainsong Psalter* (New York: The Church Hymnal Corporation, 1988).

3. James E. Barrett, *The Psalmnary: Gradual Psalms for Cantor and Congregation* (Helena, Mont.: The Hymnary Press, 1982).

4. *The Hymnal 1982: Service Music, Accompaniment Edition Volume 1* (New York: The Church Hymnal Corporation, 1985).

5. Alec Wyton, *The Anglican Chant Psalter* (New York: The Church Hymnal Corporation, 1987).

6. John Eaton, *The Psalms Come Alive: Capturing the Voice & Art of Israel's Songs* (Downers Grove, Ill.: InterVarsity, 1984), 88.

7. Suzanne Haik-Vantoura's findings were first published in her monumental work *The Music of the Bible Revealed* (1976). Her claim to have deciphered both the biblical "psalmodic" (Psalms, Proverbs, and Job) and "prosodic" (all other books of the Old Testament) musical accentual markings makes her work substantially different in kind from other systems of Psalm singing. Hers purports to be a restoration of the original melodies of the Bible—no small assertion! She has issued four recordings and numerous musical transcriptions including the melodies of all one hundred fifty psalms. A revised edition of her book has been published in English (*The Music of the Bible Revealed*, trans. Dennis Weber; ed. John Wheeler, Berkeley: BIBAL Press/King David's Harp, Inc., 1991). Several articles in English by Haik-Vantoura and by her American associate John Wheeler are also available. All of these may be obtained from John Wheeler, King David's Harp, Inc., 795 44th Ave., San Francisco, Calif. 94121-3305.

Haik-Vantoura and Wheeler point out that in antiquity the Psalms as well as all other Old Testament texts were universally sung, not spoken, when rendered in public. Internal evidence compiled by Haik-Vantoura indicates that text and melody (of every psalm and prose text) were simultaneously created by the same author as a "gestalt": an inspired "text-melody," to use her phrase. Interestingly, the psalms ascribed to various authors—David, Asaph, Moses, Solomon, the Sons of Korah, and so on—show indications in their "text-melodies" of the differing personalities of their authors. This, notes Haik-Vantoura, would be in keeping with the ancient practice of every poet being, by definition, a "poet-melodist": one whose melodies were created to help bring out the full sense of the words. Hence, in order to comprehend the meaning most fully, the music of the text must be included.

Furthermore, Haik-Vantoura believes the music she has discovered in the Hebrew Masoretic manuscripts go all the way back to Moses. If this is true, there is raised the possibility of a music divinely inspired in the same sense that the text is inspired. The importance of this for the twenty-first century church can hardly be overestimated. A "God-breathed" music would be an astounding discovery and would put this music in a category commensurate with special revelation.

8. See J. Robert Carroll, *A Guide to Gelineau Psalmody* (Toledo, Oh.: Gregorian Institute of America) and Joseph Gelineau, *Thirty Psalms and A Canticle* (Chicago: G.I.A. Publications Inc., 1957).

9. See *Music from Taizé* (Chicago: G.I.A. Publications Inc., n.d.).

10. Evertt Frese, *Advent Psalms* (Washington, D.C.: NPM Publications, 1985).

11. John Erickson, *Psalms for Singing* (Nashville: The Upper Room, 1984).

12. *Psalms For the Cantor* (Schiller Park, Ill.: World Library Publications, Inc., 1985).

13. Christopher L. Webber, *A New Metrical Psalter* (New York: The Church Hymnal Corporation, 1986).

14. Walford Davies and Harvey Grace, *Music and Worship*, 3rd ed. (London: Eyre and Spottiswoode, 1948), 111.

15. For further information concerning hymn singing see: James R. Sydnor, *Hymns and Their Uses* (Carol Stream, Ill.: Agape, 1982), idem, *Hymns: A Congregational Study* (Carol Stream, Ill.: Agape, 1982), and Alice Parker, *Creative Hymn Singing*, 2nd ed. (Chapel Hill, N.C.: Hinshaw Music, 1976).

16. *The Hymnal 1982* (New York: The Church Hymnal Corporation, 1985).

17. William J. Reynolds, *Congregational Singing* (Nashville: Convention, 1975). Reynolds gives suggested tempi for every hymn in the Baptist Hymnal.

18. Parker, *Creative Hymn Singing*, 5.

19. "Come, Holy Ghost, Our Souls Inspire," *The Hymnal 1982*, 504.

20. "Creator of the Stars of Night," *The Hymnal 1982*, 60.

21. "Come, Thou Almighty King," *The Hymnal 1982*, 365.

22. Homer Rodeheaver and Charles B. Ford, Jr., *Song Leadership* (Winona Lake, Ind.: Rodeheaver Hall-Mack Co., 1941), 21.

23. Research Committee Report of the Hymn Society of America, *The Hymn* 29 (January 1978): 37.

24. See Donald P. Hustad, "Let's Not Just Praise the Lord," *Christianity Today* (6 November 1987), 28.

25. Matthew 6:5,6 (RSV).

26. Further information may be obtained by writing members of the American Pipe Organ Builders of America such as the Schantz, Austin, Moller, or Reuter organ companies and asking for the APOBA pamphlet on acoustics. Also, the American Guild of Organists (New York) has made available "Acoustics in Worship Spaces" (pamphlet no. 6), which is excellent. Other resources include: Walter Holtkamp, "Carpeting and Singing," *The American Organist*, 20 (March 1986): 39; Carl Schalk, "A Lament for Resounding Praise," *Christian Century*, 23–30 March 1983, 269; Scott R. Riedel, "Acoustics in the Worship Space: Church Music Pamphlet Series," (St. Louis: Concordia, n.d.)

Conclusion

In Summary

In these pages we have held that the chief purpose of church music is to mature the saints of God in holistic spirituality. It is a critical mission, one too often and easily derailed by allowing music to capitulate to what we have termed the "spirit of our age"—selfism. When the focus of music in worship is the pleasuring of self, the first commandment, "You shall have no other gods before me" is broken. Worship becomes idolatrous because in focusing on self we become our own gods.

The suggested corrective to narcissistic worship is biblical discipline. The forms which comprise worship should, among other things, be disciplined or discipled forms in order to bring about maturity. Consequently, music in worship must be discipled, a state achieved through the use of disciplined principles of composition. In addition, the church music program must be a discipling ministry, actively promoting maturity in the congregation by taking seriously its mission to help the assembly grow in God. The ultimate reason for this ministry's very existence is not to make art or to make people feel good, but it is to help the believer grow out of infancy.

When music affirms theistic values in its musical form and textual content, it exerts a positive influence on people. But when it embraces contrary assumptions, producing music which is pleasure-driven, pop-oriented, and shallow, it contributes further to the downward slide of our solipsistic society. Six hundred years in the making, culture's swing from theocentricity to anthropocentricity must be resisted. The worldview of each piece of music will be conveyed consciously or unconsciously. It is often said, "We don't change the gospel, just the packaging." Not so. The musical "package" affirms or denies gospel content. The goodness and rightness of the musical form affirms or denies the goodness and rightness of the textual content. Music in church is a change agent. When it affirms integrity and creativity it becomes everything the Christian faith stands for. Good church music is the gospel in musical action—a musical analogy of the gospel. Poor church music denies the gospel. Because of music's ability to influence people, therefore, the church must use wisdom in its musical choices.

A New Direction

Reestablishing Theistic Standards

It is obvious that we need a new direction for church music in the twenty-first century. Moving away from theistic principles to secular humanistic ones has brought much misguided cultural accommodation. The issue here is broader than music. It extends to value. On what will we base our lives, our ministries, our churches, our music? Will it be on a culture which has extensively repudiated Christian values, or on a Christianity requiring repudiation of secular society's value system? Too often we want it both ways. Tom Sine notes:

> You can be sure that in the first century the disciples of Jesus Christ weren't doing Roman culture nine-to-five with church on Sundays! They understood that following Christ is a whole-life proposition that transforms life direction, values—everything. And if we are honest, we will admit that our lives really aren't that different from those of our secular counterparts. I suspect that one of the reasons we are so ineffective in evangelism is that we are so much like the people around us that we have very little to which we can call them. We hang around church buildings a little more. We abstain from a few things. But we simply aren't that different.[1]

In fact the matter goes further. Not only has secular society infiltrated our weekdays, but it has infiltrated our Sundays as well! The most sacred time of all, the hour of worship, has been invaded by the subjectivism of culture's humanistic extremes. Is it any wonder that weekdays are not all that different? When Sunday, the Lord's day, promotes the kingdom of self, we shouldn't be surprised to find it dominating the entire landscape.

The biblical preoccupation is with "doing" the truth across the broad spectrum of life. One never finds in scripture a system of belief apart from right action. Proper belief is always worked out in good deeds and does not apply just to ethics or morality. It applies to everything, aesthetics included. Our embracing of Christianity means that even music must be done truthfully—meaning rightfully, with good craftsmanship and technique.

Hence, if music is to be disciplined by biblical precepts, we cannot agree that doing whatever we wish is a possibility. An adherence to scripture means there is a limit beyond which we cannot go. Principles of right action must be upheld. The church has a biblical obligation to affirm right usage and shun wrong usage. We can no longer stick our musical/religious heads into the sand and naively assume that anything musically done in the name of religion is automatically justified. If Jesus is the truth, and as Christians we say he lives in us, we had better make sure that our actions—our musical doing—support the universal truth of the Christ of whom we sing.

In the pluralistic society in which we live, it would be well for the church to pull back from society's ambiguous attitude toward standards. After all, authority (God and scripture) is the basis on which our house is built. Take that basis away and we end up with sandcastles or fairy tales. The church cannot practice the mores of the wider culture and still be thoroughly and distinctively Christian. While the church may still be religious, it will no longer be Christian—not even if the names Jehovah, Jesus, or Holy Spirit are invoked. The working principles of a completely relativistic egalitarianism are alien to Christianity. Radical obedience needs to be revived. It is God who must be enthroned as King of kings and Lord of lords. The self must bend the knee.

It is mandatory that worship be the focal point of such a revival, without question the most important activity of the church. Individuals grow along the lines established in worship. Thus, worship music must change its focus from pleasure to discipleship, becoming more lean and austere, and it must be chosen for its ability to disciple and discipline through its astringency and asceticism.

The musical examples included in this book represent just a small beginning. There is no dearth of disciplined composition for congregations, choirs, or soloists. The music of the Middle Ages is not without a counterpart in the twentieth century. Quality church music is there for all who would avail themselves of it.[2]

An Ascetic Bent

The overarching principle of a discipling music ministry is conservatism. We must retard the advance of culture's more fleshly manifestations. Temperance will keep us from endorsing uncritically every philosophic whim and musical aberration of our secular age, yet it will encourage the truly creative gift to flourish. Neither total repudiation of the world nor indulgent acceptance of it can be the appropriate stance of the Christian musician. But if the musician of the twenty-first century is to err, let it be on the side of moderation. Now is time for the pendulum to swing back toward the emphasis of the Middle Ages, toward a more straightforward, austere, and ascetic view of God as King.

The Great Commission of Matthew 28:19, 20 gives us important direction. The imperative form of the phrase "to make disciples" shows the intent of Jesus' statement. As "we are in the world" or "as we are going along in the world," we are to make (the imperative form) disciples, teaching them to obey our Lord's commands. We are to disciple men and women in the Christian life; a discipleship complete and holistic, touching everything we are and do.

Church music must be in earnest over its role as discipler. This is critical, since we just fool ourselves if we attempt to disciple people by teaching them Christian concepts (content) without a parallel understanding that a change in lifestyle (form) is necessary. And music in worship is one of the forms of the Christian life. If we continue to use the undisciplined music of a hedonistic society in worship (Christian pop), we will never have mature Christians, no matter how we rationalize such usage. The gulf between faith and works, belief and practice, is just too wide. After all, actions, even musical ones, are a Christian's true and actual lived-out theology.

The meaning that art forms have within a society will change as culture changes. The criteria for their use in worship ought never be their acceptance or popularity, but the discipling meaning and potential which they hold for the assembly. Music which is obviously adamic and fleshly in nature has no discipling potential, but music which is modest, sober, and shows integrity does. Through music as gospel analogue, congregations are discipled.

Focusing church music on discipling is a big task given the contemporary mind set. But the twenty-first century needs this emphasis, since the church cannot afford to dismiss the call to a more ascetic Christianity any longer. Instead of idly following the trends of the general culture, the church should move into culture with a clear and radically different alternative, heralding a more disciplined approach to Christian living.

Even as the twentieth century has continued to unravel the tightly knit influence of God over human life, so the next century must reestablish it. Church musicians have a major role to play because of the power and control art forms enjoy over contemporary society. Music ministers will need a special measure of fortitude to stand by decisions they know to be in the best long-term interest of their people. Designing worship to be biblically sound and less faddish, straightforward and less manipulative, ascetic rather than indulgent, honest and less showy (pretentious), God-centric and not ego-centric, more wholesome (edifying) than entertaining, will call for some rugged changes. Strong decisions will need equally strong implementation. Music as a discipling agent is a far cry from what congregations expect music to be. They may very well not like it at all, but a discipling music ministry is not predicated upon fleshly enjoyment, but upon people's need to grow into the likeness of Jesus. When faced with a complaining parishioner who wanted to know why the congregation was not allowed a particular kind of music in worship, the late Dr. Erik Routley simply replied, "You can't have it because it is not good for you."

Pessimism is always tempting. Living in a world which has alienated itself from godly precepts and worshiping in a church which itself has so often succumbed to the enticing beck and call of the world do not give any of us (congregation, pastor, or musicians) cause for an easy, rosy, unthinking optimism. But there is hope. "Greater is He that is in you, than he that is in the world."[3] Hope does not spring from our ability to right wrong, but from God's ability to work through dedicated vessels. We cannot rely upon our own strength to wrestle with principalities and powers. Only God can win this battle. So our hope comes from God, because faith in him keeps us from despair. If we are steadfast, willing to pay the cost of being a disciple, God will use us as channels of his grace and glory.

Disciples are joyful people, their joy founded in Christ who calls them to do right. When focused inwardly on oneself, joy turns into self-centered, ego-indulgent pleasure. Musical fun, frivolity, amusement, superficiality, and escape do not express maturity, nor do such forms help people become mature. We need to avoid them.

A music ministry which attempts to mature believers will not be easy. Both accomplishments and disappointments are bound to accompany such a task. But the Great Commission not only gives us a mandate to make disciples in the twenty-first century, it assures us that "lo, I am with you alway, *even* unto the end of the world. Amen."[4]

Notes

1. Tom Sine, *Why Settle for More and Miss the Best?* (Waco: Word Publishing Co., 1987), 109.
2. A few of the many contemporary composers whose work espouses a more disciplined approach to composition useful in a maturing music ministry are Carl Schalk, Hugo Distler, Ralph Vaughan Williams, Healey Willan, Jan Bender, David Willcocks, Gerald Near, Leo Sowerby, Knut Nystedt, Daniel Pinkham, and Paul Bunjes.
3. 1 John 4:4 (KJV).
4. Matthew 28:20 (KJV).